SALINGER

THE CATCHER IN THE RYE & NINE STORIES

NOTES

COLES EDITORIAL BOARD

Bound to stay open

Publisher's Note

Otabind (Ota-bind). This book has been bound using the patented Otabind process. You can open this book at any page, gently run your finger down the spine, and the pages will lie flat.

ABOUT COLES NOTES

COLES NOTES have been an indispensible aid to students on five continents since 1948.

COLES NOTES are available for a wide range of individual literary works. Clear, concise explanations and insights are provided along with interesting interpretations and evaluations.

Proper use of COLES NOTES will allow the student to pay greater attention to lectures and spend less time taking notes. This will result in a broader understanding of the work being studied and will free the student for increased participation in discussions.

COLES NOTES are an invaluable aid for review and exam preparation as well as an invitation to explore different interpretive paths.

COLES NOTES are written by experts in their fields. It should be noted that any literary judgement expressed herein is just that – the judgement of one school of thought. Interpretations that diverge from, or totally disagree with any criticism may be equally valid.

COLES NOTES are designed to supplement the text and are not intended as a substitute for reading the text itself. Use of the NOTES will serve not only to clarify the work being studied, but should enhance the readers enjoyment of the topic.

ISBN 0-7740-3257-X

© COPYRIGHT 2000 AND PUBLISHED BY
COLES PUBLISHING COMPANY
TORONTO - CANADA
PRINTED IN CANADA

Manufactured by Webcom Limited
Cover finish: Webcom's Exclusive **DURACOAT**

CONTENTS

J.D. Salinger: Life and Works

In J.D. Salinger's novel *The Catcher in the Rye*, the hero, Holden Caulfield, muses at one point upon the possibility of escaping from the world of confusion and "phonies" as that world exists in the tense, vulgar life of New York City. Holden dreams of fleeing to the West, where he plans to live as a deaf mute. In his Utopia, he intends to allow few visitors, and he plans to enforce a strict code of ethics under which no one will ever be able to do anything "phony."

In *The Catcher*, Holden eventually recognizes that there is no place in the world, East or West, that guarantees peace and security. Ironically, however, Holden's creator has spent a good part of his adult life gradually withdrawing from the coarse world that Holden learns he must come to terms with. To add to the irony, Salinger, even in the depths of his withdrawal, preaches the need of the artist to perform and to create, not for the exceptional man, but for the vulgar, ordinary human being. In his story "Zooey," Salinger lets Zooey make this point when he tells his sister Franny that she shouldn't complain about the stupidity of audiences. Instead she should remember The Fat Lady — a vulgar, thick-legged, cancerous creature who plays the radio full blast all day long — and should perform well for The Fat Lady because the universe is made up of Fat Ladies.

This curious, paradoxical man was born Jerome David Salinger on January 1, 1919, the second child and only son of a prosperous Jewish father (Sol Salinger) and a Christian mother (Miriam Jillich Salinger). As a child, J.D. Salinger (or Sonny as he was called) was fond of tennis, pool and dramatics, but on the whole he preferred long, lonely walks to childhood sports and games. From the beginning he was shy and withdrawn, with a love for words, story-telling, and play-acting.

Salinger went to school in Manhattan where he was an average student with an average I.Q. (tested at 104). At the age of 13 he was enrolled in the McBurney School, a highly selective private school in Manhattan. He did so poorly there that he was transferred, a year later, to Valley Forge Military Academy. There his I.Q. was again tested (the 115 result was in the higher range of average), and he did satisfactory work in his studies. At Valley Forge, Salinger learned the beginnings of self-discipline, even though he did occasionally violate the rules of the school by sneaking away, after lights out, to have a beer or two at a nearby tavern. In addition Salinger became more outgoing than he had ever been before, and the numerous extracurricular activities in which he participated made him a Big Man on Campus.

During this time, Salinger absorbed much of the material he was to use in *The Catcher in the Rye*: for instance, one of Salinger's classmates committed suicide, like James Castle, by jumping from a window; and the psychological problems of another classmate led to his being expelled, like Holden Caulfield, from school. Most important of all, Salinger began to dream of literary fame and fortune (most especially through selling stories to Hollywood) and to work actively toward a literary career. At times, after lights out, he used a flashlight under his blanket to continue his reading and writing. During his senior year he became literary editor of the school yearbook, *Crossed Sabres*, and in June, 1936, he contributed a sentimental poem to commemorate The Last Parade. The poem was set to music and is still sung on graduation day.

Though he spent brief periods of time at New York University and Ursinus College, Salinger had little interest in continuing his formal education beyond high school. His interest in writing, however, led him in 1938 to enroll in a course in short-story writing at Columbia University. The course was taught by Whit Burnett, the editor of *Story* magazine. He was so impressed with Salinger's story "The Young Folks" that he published it in the March, 1940, issue of *Story*. After that initial success, Salinger began to appear in a number of the better-paying American magazines. In 1948 he signed a contract with *The New Yorker*. In that magazine, usually considered the best-paying American market for serious creative writing, Salinger has published most of his short fiction since 1948.

Few biographical details remain to be noted. One of the most important of these concerns Salinger's wartime service. Initially, because of a minor heart condition, he was given a deferred draft classification. Apparently that rating bothered him for he sought advice from Valley Forge Military Academy as to the part he might play in the war effort. His problem was solved in 1942 when selective service standards were slightly lowered. Soon after Salinger was drafted. During his early months of training and service he did clerical work and wrote publicity releases. On his week-end passes he often rented a secluded hotel room and worked on his own writing. In late 1943 Salinger was assigned to the Intelligence Corps of the Fourth Infantry Division and after a period of training in Devonshire, England, he participated in the European invasion of June 6, 1944. Through five campaigns, including the Battle of the Bulge, Salinger served as an intelligence agent seeking by interrogation to expose Nazi agents and intrigue. Yet when Salinger, in 1944, contributed $200 to *Story* magazine to be used in aiding young writers, he noted that he was "still writing whenever I can find the time. . . ."

With the end of World War II Salinger returned to America. For a while he lived with his parents in New York, and during this time he pursued Manhattan girls and Oriental philosophy (Zen Buddhism) with equal enthusiasm. When New York and Greenwich Village began to pall, he began a series of retreats, to Tarrytown, New York, to Westport, Connecticut, and to Cornish, New Hampshire. For a while in New Hampshire, Salinger was a sociable man, so fond of local high-school youngsters that he entertained them with record parties at his hilltop home and became a familiar figure at their local hangouts. During this period Salinger became acquainted with a few members of the Dartmouth College faculty, and at a cocktail party he met an attractive Radcliffe student named Claire Douglas (the girl on whom he modeled the heroine of his story "Franny"). Salinger and Miss Douglas became close friends (a common bond was their interest in mysticism), but their intimacy was shattered when Miss Douglas suddenly married another man. Soon after this "betrayal," as Salinger may have conceived it, Salinger put a high fence around his home, and his friendship with the local townspeople, including the high-school gang, ceased completely.

Miss Douglas' marital choice, considering her cast of mind, was a strange one — a student at Harvard Business School — and the marriage lasted but a brief time. In 1955, soon after her divorce, she and Salinger were married, but the high fence around Salinger's home remained.

Today Salinger seems content to live with his wife and two children behind his high wall. He seems uninterested in the coarser realities of the Fat Lady. In his seclusion, the tall, pale, author shies away from all publicity. He resents all scholarly

3

interest in his work, ignores scholar's queries, is said to feel that he alone has any proper right to analyze his writing, and scorns republication or dramatization of his work. Symbolic of Salinger's withdrawal is the fact that *Time* magazine, when it published a feature story on him in 1961, used a picture of his mailbox, instead of his portrait, to adorn the magazine cover.

In his art, Salinger rejects contempt of the masses, but his life shows how sympathetic these ideas are to him. Rather ironically, as he has drawn further and further from the common herd, he has found himself less and less able to write well enough to satisfy his own aims. Thus he goes each day to the small, concrete, sky-lighted cell, some hundred yards distant from his home, that he uses as his study. There he puts in his working days, but since his marriage he has published little. Possibly one reason he has become indifferent to publication is that he sees such acts as egoistic ones that link him to the mob he claims to love but partially despises. His heroine Franny, when she thinks of giving up the stage, makes this point when she claims that she is sickened and disgusted by ego, her own and everyone else's, and repelled by the universal drive to *get somewhere*.

Franny is taught differently by her brother Zooey, but perhaps Zooey's arguments no longer convince J.D. Salinger.

Aside from *The Catcher in the Rye*, Salinger has collected the writing he wishes to preserve in a collection of short stories, *Nine Stories*; the short novels "Franny" and "Zooey" in a one-volume edition; and the short novels "Raise High the Roof Beam, Carpenters" and "Seymour, an Introduction" in a one-volume edition.

In these works Salinger dramatizes his interest in children (especially sensitive, precocious ones); his revulsion for the rat race in which sophisticated adults pass their days; and his obsession with the adult destinies of a family of child prodigies who once starred in a radio program called "It's a Wise Child." One of the better short stories is "For Esmé — with Love and Squalor." Drawing upon his own war-time training in England, Salinger tells of a meeting that an American soldier has with a precocious, warm-hearted young English girl. The child, whose father has been killed in the war and whose mother has recently died, asks the soldier, and potential writer, to write a story for her someday — one that she wishes to be squalid and touching.

4

"Pretty Mouth and Green My Eyes" reveals Salinger's distaste for the sophisticated life. It explores a triangular relationship in which a man torn between love and hatred for his "animal" wife seeks advice from the very friend who is cuckolding him. In "Teddy", Salinger combines his interest in precocious children and repulsive adults. The adults are Teddy's parents, and both of them are spiteful creatures whose squabbles reveal them to be what Salinger would call spiritual tramps. Teddy, on the other hand, is a young mystic who claims to despise emotions but who is still sensitive to the reactions of his parents. He writes a number of entries in his diary, one of which is that some strange event will possibly happen to him on the day of the tale. One legitimate conclusion to the puzzling, indefinite end of the story is that Teddy has desired death rather than a boring life in an American body as the son of coarse and vulgar parents, and for that reason he has decided to fulfill the premonition which he had known.

In addition to such stories as these, Salinger has written a number of tales about the Glass family. The parents of this family are an Irish mother, Bessie Gallagher Glass, and a Jewish father, Les Glass. This former song and dance vaudeville team has produced seven children, all of whom have exhibited their charm and knowledge at one time or another on a radio show called "It's a Wise Child." The children, whose birth dates cover the span from 1918-1934, are Seymour, Buddy, Boo-Boo, the twins Waker and Walt, Zooey, and Franny. Seymour, the eldest, seems to be, in Salinger's eyes, both an intellectual (he took his Ph.D. at the age of 21) and an enigmatic saint, and his interest in Zen Buddhism, as well as the mystery of his suicide, hovers continually in the family conscience. Buddy, who was born in the same year as Salinger and whom Salinger has described as his "alter-ego," is the writer of the family; he makes his living, without great happiness, by teaching unintelligent girls in a junior college in up-state New York. Boo-Boo is the wife of a young man named Tannenbaum and the mother of three children. Walt was killed in a freak explosion during World War II, and his twin brother Waker is a Catholic priest. Zooey is a handsome, even beautiful, television actor. Franny, the baby of the family, is a college student who has acted in summer stock and shown remarkable talent.

Three of Salinger's stories in *Nine Stories*, and all the short novels he has published in volume form, dramatize parts of this saga of the Glass family. "A Perfect Day for Bananafish" tells of the last few hours that Seymour Glass lived before he put a bullet in his forehead. "Down at the Dinghy" dramatizes Boo-Boo Glass's attempt to soothe the feelings of her young son Lionel after a traumatic experience. "Uncle Wiggily in Connecticut," which Hollywood made into a sentimental movie called "My Foolish Heart" (starring Susan Hayward and Dana Andrews), dramatizes the impact of Walt Glass upon a young matron's heart. After Walt's war-time death, the woman, Eloise, marries and has a child, but she is unable to forget Walt's grace and humor, and her life turns sour.

Salinger's most ambitious works, aside from *The Catcher*, have been his four short novels about the Glass family, and he apparently plans even more Glass material. Two of these short novels, "Raise High the Roof Beam, Carpenters" and "Seymour — an Introduction," are about the family poet and seer, Seymour, the eldest of the Glass children. "Raise High" is a relatively conventional story (though it features a number of intrusive asides by the narrator) in which Buddy Glass tells his memories of the day of his brother Seymour's wedding.

In "Seymour — an Introduction," Buddy Glass again tries to pierce the mystery of Seymour's personality. He does this in a most garrulous fashion and with an outpouring of stylistic mannerisms implying an almost religious need of his to come close to the reader and intimately reveal all the possible details of Seymour's dress, manners, poetry, and ideas. In describing these things, Buddy seems to be struggling with a task beyond his abilities, so that his physical powers are tested to their utmost, and he constantly must break off the description to rest and to sleep. The final inference is that the "Introduction" is Buddy's attempt to still the ghost of Seymour by hand-to-hand struggle, so that Buddy himself may come into being as his own man. When, however, he quits writing about Seymour — for "Seymour" is a formless story that stops rather than ends — Seymour is still with him, reminding Buddy of the divine light that shines in even the dullest of humankind.

In the two other short novels, Salinger turns to the younger Glass children. "Franny," which set college campuses buzzing on its publication in 1955, is the satirical tale of the beginning of a weekend campus date. The big campus question at the time of the story's publication was whether Franny was pregnant — and the point of the story is the contrast between her mentality and that of her date. Intellectual communication between them was impossible. (Salinger had, of course, explored a similar contrast in "Raise High the Roof Beam, Carpenters." In that story, he made the incommunicability between Seymour and his fiancée explicit.)

In the last of these Glass stories, "Zooey," Salinger continues the tale of Franny. This last tale is narrated by Buddy Glass, and it tells of the efforts of Franny's brother Zooey to bring her back from her despair to a belief in the worth and meaningfulness of human endeavor. The message Zooey conveys is that one should accept the reality that egotism is the reason for human striving and that imperfect human beings live everywhere on earth.

Despite their occasional mannerisms, cuteness, narcissism, and sentimentality, these minor works of Salinger are interesting in themselves, but even more for the light they throw on *The Catcher in the Rye*. Through them, the reader can see the themes that dominate *The Catcher*: the need for love; the search for something other than self in which to believe; the problem of the sensitive man's inability to communicate with his fellows; the contempt for purely materialistic goals and for phoniness wherever it is to be found; the need to accept, and even love, one's fellows despite their imperfections; and finally the knowledge that there is no escape, in this world, from the ugliness which is reality, which is life.

Introduction to *The Catcher in the Rye*

When *The Catcher in the Rye* made its appearance in 1951, J.D. Salinger was heralded as the spokesman of a new generation. "Salinger," said one critic, "has spoken with more magic, particularly to the young, than any other U.S. writer since World War II." It is hard to judge the full effect of Salinger on his readership, but one can assess some of the reasons for the literary attention that has centered around his first and only full-length novel to date.

Holden Caulfield's protests and barbed comments about life have become familiar conversation in high schools and college campuses throughout the country. His target is a large one and his animosity is directed towards everything and anything in our culture that could be damned with his favorite word "phony."

Holden Caulfield claims a position that no other character in contemporary literature can rival. The students' sense of identity with Holden Caulfield is easy to explain because Holden shares many of their conflicts with the adult world. His prejudices are honest and are directed mostly towards a society suffering from "insufficient love." The sardonic tone which he uses to zero in on his targets has produced a wit that is, as one critic termed it, "half humorous and half agonizing."

Holden Caulfield personifies the sensitive individual at bay in a crass and superficial world. He sees his society for what it is, and he longs for what he wants it to be. Holden is essentially a misfit. He has managed to flunk out of one school after another with a distinctive blend of indifference and ease. He finds himself alienated from a society which he sees as short on compassion but overloaded with pretense and sham. He protests against a world where even the price of a set of luggage is enough to separate school roommates, where ambitions are hollow, and the purpose of school is to gather up sufficient wisdom (knowledge) so that someday you can buy a long, sleek, shiny Cadillac. Holden objects to the make-believe concern about the school's football team. He rebels against the pseudo-sophisticated conversations about girls, sex and liquor that seem to be the only subjects his schoolmates find meaningful.

Holden's protests supersede the social and academic life around him, for he finds that the adult world is little better. He suffers over the adult world's preoccupation with material things rather than with the feelings of one person for another. He balks at New York congestion, and a world that is too mechanical and organized. He seethes in nightclubs filled with phonies who are ecstatic over their proximity to would-be celebrities who entertain at these places. Holden is repelled, also, by the social climbers who warm up during a telephone conversation only after the mention of Princeton, or a similarly appreciated university.

Holden's objections towards parental and school authority, as well as the phony ideas and hollow ambitions that tarnish a world he wishes to love, have become stock criticisms of the day. Yet the vigor and the satire with which he attacks his targets often have brought upon both the character and the author the wrath of critics searching for weaknesses in his stand. Maxwell Geismar acknowledges that *The Catcher in the Rye* is a protest, to be sure, against both the academic and social conformity of its period. But what does it argue *for*? What Holden is asking for in his rebellion, and through his futile search for companionship and the final despair that brings him close to mental collapse, is a world where there is more love and more honesty among men. When Holden finds that he is running out of people to whom he can turn and his determination to escape the crass world around him becomes firmer in his mind, he calls on one of his favorite teachers and family friends who reminds him that he is ". . . not the first person who was ever confused and frightened and sickened by human behavior." The reader may take the view of Holden's best-loved companion and younger sister, Phoebe, who sees her brother not really ". . . liking anything that's happening."

It does not matter whether or not the reader sides with Holden and shares his views, or admires his refusal to compromise. It is important to realize that before any social criticism can be taken seriously it must offer some alternative or perhaps some affirmation to balance the maladies such as those which Holden attacks with such satire and candor. Holden tells Phoebe that he likes his dead brother, Allie, who possessed the ability to combine both intelligence and compassion. Holden also holds in deep respect the memory of a previous classmate who jumped to his death from a dormitory window rather than be bullied into retracting a statement. These seem to be the only people who have meant anything to Holden.

In the final analysis, Holden's criticisms do not rest solely with a world that bulges with phonies and pretense so much as it rests with man's dilemma. Holden is caught in that adolescent twilight zone between the past security of childhood innocence and the inevitable steps of growing up, growing old, and, somewhere in the maturing process, facing eventual death. He is not only repulsed by the social forces brought to bear upon the adults of this world but depressed by the physical deterioration which comes with age. He sees Mr. Spencer, his history teacher, as a senile man who causes one to question the current and continuing purpose of his (Mr. Spencer's) life. Holden finds Mr. Spencer's appearance as well as his physical surroundings (in his room) unpleasant, with pills and medicines scattered all over, and a distinct odor of Vicks Nose Drops permeating everything. Holden sees Mr. Spencer in his bathrobe and pajamas and finds this a most depressing sight. All of Holden's thought processes indicate his developing coming-to-grips with reality (i.e., growing up, assuming responsibility, growing old, and somewhere deep inside, the possibility of dying). Can Holden cope with this knowledge?

Holden Caulfiled is more than just a satirist; through all his experiences he remains compassionate. Whether his contemporaries are indifferent, insufferable boors or girls he remembers best because they keep their kings in the back row during games of checkers, Holden has a tenderness towards their isolation and suffering. This compassion extends to include everyone from the unpopular and obnoxious Ackley at Pencey Prep to mothers who ask all those stupid questions when buying ice skates; as well as to prostitutes who shake him down after he finds himself too embarrassed and too sympathetic towards their plight to take them to bed.

It is not the nature of Holden Caulfield's protests which makes *The Catcher in the Rye* such a significant novel. Its real achievement rests with the manner in which J.D. Salinger has developed his novel. The eye for detail and the ear for dialogue are always there. This is a work which becomes real through the use of the everyday vernacular speech of the adolescent. Holden's story is a magnificent blend of perception, humor and despair that breathes and pulses and evokes sensation. It is life.

Arthur Mizener links Salinger with Mark Twain, Ring Lardner and Ernest Hemingway as writers who ". . . depend more than most writers on the fine shading of style to convey meaning." Mizener points out that all three pride themselves on their use of ". . . homely American speech with great accuracy, but were saying things with it that few homely Americans are wholly conscious of." In an essay that is excellent for its thoroughness, Donald Costello emphasizes that the personal idiosyncrasies of Holden's speech are in ". . . keeping with the general teenage language . . . an artistic rendering of a type of informal colloquial teenage American spoken speech. It is strongly typical and trite, yet often somewhat individual; it is crude and slangy and imprecise, imitative yet occasionally imaginative, and affected towards standardization by the strong efforts of schools."

The following lines which open *The Catcher in the Rye* are typical examples of Salinger's skill in reconstructing this "teen-age language."

> If you really want to hear about it, the first thing you'll probably want to know is where I was born, and what my lousy childhood was like, and how my parents were occupied . . . . and all that David Copperfield kind of crap. . . . my parents would have about two hemorrhages apiece if I told anything pretty personal about them.

Holden Caulfield often has been compared to Mark Twain's Huckleberry Finn. He and Holden Caulfield have had their fill of what Huck calls "sivilization," both wish to turn their backs on society and to retreat to nature and a life that is not so complicated. Both are rebels and both possess a fierce sense of justice and morality. Such a comparison, particularly in terms of thought and speech, is an accurate one and serves as an indication that J.D. Salinger's Holden Caulfield stands beside Huck Finn as one of ". . . two youthful travelers who have earned their passports to literary immortality."

Alfred Kazin has said that "Above all, he (Salinger) is a favorite with the audience of students, student intellectuals, instructors and generally literary, sensitive and sophisticated young people who respond to him with a consciousness that he speaks for them and virtually *to* them, in a language that is peculiarly honest and their own, with a view of things that captures their most secret judgments of the world." Caulfield does more than speak to his readers. He represents them, and he does so by embellishing their views, their feelings and their mannerisms, ultimately bringing his readers to the realization that there is something of Caulfield in all of us. This evocation of our own "insides" is what we will find meaningful as we read *The Catcher in the Rye*.

Plot Summary

Holden Caulfield is a prep school student who has had trouble with every school he has attended: first the Whooton School, then Elkton Hills, and now Pencey. As the novel begins, Holden is in a psychiatric hospital in California and prepares to tell his story to a psychoanalyst at that institution. But the analyst is also the reader, and Holden addresses each person who reads the novel in a very intimate manner.

His story takes place in a short period of time — several days. He begins with his expulsion from the Pencey School where he has flunked four out of five subjects. He does not like the teachers, nor does he enjoy the students: they are snobby, of wealthy families, and have an air of phoniness about them. Phony people are Holden's enemies, he will do anything to avoid them.

Holden is the manager of the Pencey fencing team. The team goes into New York City for a match, but Holden loses their foils in the subway so they are unable to compete. This means that they must return to Pennsylvania unfulfilled, and they are angry with Holden. When they arrive back on campus, there is a football game in progress. Instead of attending it with the rest of the school, Holden pays a last visit to a teacher whom he respects. Mr. Spencer lectures him on his conduct, but bids him a fond farewell.

That evening, the boy in the next room to Holden's in the dormitory comes over to visit him. His name is Ackley and he is a terrific bore. They talk about Pencey, and Holden believes that it is a school of phonies.

Later, Holden's roommate Stradlater comes in. He is a sexy, virile athlete who asks Holden to write a composition for one of his courses. He has a date with Jane Gallagher that evening and does not have time to write it himself. Holden is very depressed about his roommate's date. Jane Gallagher was one of Holden's friends and he does not want her to be taken advantage of by Stradlater. Throughout the novel, Jane will represent Holden's ideal of purity and unspoiled female companionship, but he is unable to see her or have contact with her.

Holden writes Stradlater's composition on a subject very dear to him: his brother Allie's baseball mitt. Holden describes his younger brother, who died of leukemia, with great love.

Allie was the kind of kid who wrote verses of poetry on his baseball mitt so that he could entertain himself in the field when no one was at bat. Holden is moved by this and describes it in the essay. When Stradlater returns from his date, he is angered by Holden's choice of topics and Holden is worried about Stradlater's treatment of Jane. The two fight and Holden is pushed to the floor with a bloody nose.

Holden decides to leave Pencey school instead of waiting until Wednesday, when the school closes for Christmas. He takes the train to his home in New York but cannot go directly to his parents' apartment: they are not expecting him home until Wednesday and, since they know nothing of his expulsion from Pencey, he prefers that they find it out in his absence. So he goes to a cheap hotel, the Edmont, and enters a dreary marathon of sordid events which ultimately bring his depression to a head. From this point until the end of the novel, Holden relates what happens to him before he is admitted to the mental hospital.

At the Edmont, he is offered a prostitute by the shady elevator man. The woman comes to Holden's room but he is too nervous and depressed to have sex, so he sends her off. She complains that he hasn't paid enough but she eventually leaves. Later, the man returns with the prostitute and beats Holden up in order to get more money from him.

The next day, Holden calls up Sally Hayes, a sometime friend, and makes a theater date for that afternoon. In the meantime, he walks down Broadway looking for a special record for his sister Phoebe, whom he adores. He overhears a little boy walking by the curb and singing a verse from a Robert Burns poem: "If a body catch a body coming through the rye." This makes Holden happy and he decides, later on, that his role in life is to help innocent children resist the vulgarity of adult civilization. He seems himself as someone who will catch them before they fall over the cliff of evil, and this explains the novel's title: he will be the catcher in a field of rye.

Holden and Sally attend the theater. He dislikes the phoniness of actors and of the know-it-all spectators. Afterward, Holden and Sally go skating and Holden suggests they go away together for a couple of weeks. Sally thinks it is an impractical idea, they fight and Holden leaves.

He calls up Carl Luce, an arrogant school friend, and the

two meet for a drink. It proves to be another unsatisfactory encounter for Holden. Luce talks condescendingly to Holden and quickly abandons him in the bar. Holden gets very drunk, walks to Central Park, drops the record he bought for Phoebe and is saddened when it smashes into pieces. He is alone and frightened in the Park, and feels a need to see his sister.

He decides to go and see Phoebe, taking the chance that his parents might see him. They do not. But after an emotionally charged session with Phoebe, where they express their love for one another, he leaves to spend the evening in the apartment of Mr. Antolini, a former English teacher. While there, he is awakened from his sleep by Antolini's hand on his head. Alarmed by what he perceives to be a homosexual advance, Holden leaves nervously in the middle of the night.

He goes to Grand Central Station, sleeps badly for a couple of hours, then gets the idea to hitch-hike out West and find a job. He wants to see Phoebe one last time and arranges to meet her at the Metropolitan Museum of Art. She arrives with her suitcase, wanting desperately to accompany her brother, but he refuses and they have an argument. Finally, they reconcile and Holden agrees to go home to their parents' apartment with her — but not before he gets drenched in a rainstorm and becomes ill.

The novel ends with a brief concluding chapter in which Holden mentions his plans to go back to school in September. He is not sure whether he will be successful there or not, but knows that it is never possible to predict the future.

Characters in the Novel

Robert Ackley: A student at Pencey Prep, he lives in the room next to Holden.

Mr. Antolini: Holden's former English teacher at Elkton Hills.

Mal Brossard: A student at Pencey Prep.

James Castle: A student at Elkton Hills who committed suicide.

Allie Caulfield: Holden's younger brother who died of leukemia.

D.B. Caulfield: Holden's older brother who is a writer in Hollywood.

Holden Caulfield: The narrator and main character in the novel. He is 16 years old.

Mr. and Mrs. Caulfield: Holden's wealthy parents. Mr. Caulfield is a corporate lawyer.

Phoebe Caulfield: Holden's 10-year-old sister.

Jane Gallagher: A friend of Holden's. In his eyes, she is a symbol of purity.

Sally Hayes: A friend with whom Holden makes a date to go to the theater.

Carl Luce: A student Holden knew from Whooton. He meets Holden for a drink in New York City.

Lillian Simmons: An old girlfriend of D.B.'s whom Holden runs into in "Ernie's" night club.

Mr. Spencer: A History teacher at Pencey Prep.

Ward Stradlater: Holden's roommate at Pencey Prep.

Chapter by Chapter
Summaries and Commentaries

NOTE: All quotations are from *The Catcher in the Rye*, J.D. Salinger. Bantam Books, 1981.

CHAPTER 1

Summary

Holden Caulfield is the narrator of this novel. From the very beginning, he launches into a confession of events leading to his present situation in a rest home in California. He addresses the reader in a conversational and humorous tone, relating how his parents would not want him to reveal anything about them: "They're quite touchy about anything like that, especially my father." He says that they are nice, but irritable. Holden does not want this book to be autobiographical; he seeks to highlight only the important moments of his past and to tell them from his point of view, starting with what happened last Christmas.

Holden was a student at Pencey Prep School in Agerstown, Pennsylvania; one of those schools seen in classified ads which claim to turn boys into "splendid, clear-thinking young men." Holden is pleasantly sarcastic about it all, indeed, very funny, when he avows that not even the remotest kind of molding takes place at Pencey. It is a showy, foolish place to be.

The time frame of his flashback is Saturday, the day of the football game with Saxon Hall. This was a very important event for most of the students and "you were supposed to commit suicide or something if old Pencey didn't win."

Holden was not present at the game. Instead, he stood on top of Thomsen Hill and surveyed the stadium from the distance. He had been in New York City earlier that day as manager of the fencing team, but since he left all of their equipment on the subway, the team was unable to compete and had to return to Pencey. Holden stood on top of the hill and watched the two teams "bash" away at each other while he tried to feel a proper sorrow at leaving Pencey Prep. After a few minutes, Holden ran to say good-bye to his history teacher Mr. Spencer. Mr. Spencer had the flu and Holden figured he would not see him again. The teacher knew that Holden was not returning to Pencey after the holidays as he had been expelled for not applying himself and for failing four subjects.

He ran across the highway to Mr. Spencer's house, frozen by the cold weather. Mrs. Spencer opened the door and was very kind to Holden. She reported that her husband was feeling better and that Holden should go directly to his room to see him.

Commentary

Though this book is divided into chapters and has the external markings of a novel, it is in every other way a confession by the hero, Holden Caulfield, to both the reader and the psychoanalyst at Holden's California rest home.

The style is casual, conversational and engaging. It grips the reader immediately by breaking down barriers of objectivity and establishing a sense of humorous sarcasm about Holden's plight. There is no obvious attempt in this first chapter to attack or criticize the establishment. We see Holden as a sensitive, intelligent young man whose intuition and insight provide him with the necessary force to see through snobbery, arrogance and hypocrisy.

His brother D.B., to whom he alludes only briefly, is a Hollywood writer making a lot of money. Holden describes his brother as a regular writer who has enslaved himself to the ideals of Hollywood in order to make money. Holden is dedicated to truth, value and meaning; and is not interested in the status quo or social standing. His language is that of a teenager (e.g. "lousy crap," "they're as touchy as hell") but his thought patterns are considerably more intense than many of his peers. It is this disarming linguistic quality which allows him to pierce through the "phonies" — a theme which weaves through the entire book. Examples of phonies in this chapter are the Pencey School, Hollywood movies and even his own brother D.B., who "sells out" to the corporate structure of filmland.

The stylistic technique is that of the flashback. Though Salinger controls his prose very carefully, Holden's narration takes shape in the form of memories about the past, reminiscences and stream-of-consciousness, anecdotes and stories which flesh in the essence of Holden's personality. The confession begins on a Saturday afternoon prior to the beginning of the Christmas vacation at Pencey School.

CHAPTER 2

Summary

Holden describes Mr. Spencer as a stooped over 70-year-old who enjoyed the simpler things in life. He respects his teacher, even though he wonders at times why he is still alive. Mr. Spencer asks him about his conversation with Dr. Thurmer, the headmaster, and Holden replies that Thurmer spoke of life being a game, that one "should play it according to the rules." Holden shows no animosity about Thurmer's speech to him; he accepts it as part of the educator's duty. But Holden knows that life is only a game if you are on the right side, where all the "hot-shots" are.

Mr. Spencer asks Holden how his parents will respond to his expulsion from Pencey. His reply: "They'll be pretty irritated about it. . . This is about the fourth school I've gone to." Holden is 16 at the time of his conversation with Spencer (one year before the actual time of this story's narration) and confesses that he often acts much younger than his age. Then he adds that he often acts a lot older than he is, but no one notices this: "People never notice anything."

When Spencer calls Holden's parents "grand" people, the boy reacts with disgust: "There's a word I really hate. It's a phony." Spencer gives him a lecture on his work performance; he reproaches him for not doing better in history and proceeds to go through Holden's history exam with him. Spencer reminds Caulfield that he has exhibited similar behavior at other schools, namely Whooton and Elkton Hills. Holden says he left Elkton Hills, however, because he was "surrounded by phonies. They were coming in the goddam window." Holden tells Spencer that he feels little concern for his future; he believes himself to be a moron, or at least this is what he tells Spencer. Holden says he is going through a phase. As he leaves, he hears Mr. Spencer calling "good luck" to him, which he regrets: "I'd never yell 'good luck' at anybody. It sounds terrible, when you think about it."

Commentary

This chapter tells us much about Holden's personality. He is a kind, sympathetic person who cares enough about the feelings of his history teacher to pay him one last visit. He identifies many of the features associated with old people ("unhairy" legs, bumpy chests, deafness, etc.) and feels internal revulsion for them; yet he shows respect and courtesy to this man whose history lectures he has enjoyed, even though he failed the course.

Mr. Spencer is not a phony. He expects his students to do well and is disappointed when they do not. He derives pleasure from the simple things in life, such as his Navajo blanket, and he is sufficiently without pretense that he begins picking his nose in Holden's presence. But Spencer represents a transition in Holden's life; he is symbolic of Pencey School (note the similarity between Spencer and Pencey) and, as a teacher, stands for authority ("You can't stop a teacher when they want to do something"). It is as if Holden must phase himself out of Pencey in a gradual manner and Spencer represents the last meaningful contact with the establishment.

Mr. Spencer is in his early seventies, but Holden feels a closeness toward him. Perhaps it is Spencer's age that prompts him to interrogate Holden about his concern for the future. Death, the after-life and other related concerns are often foremost on the mind of many aging people, but for Holden, the future plays no role. The difference in their personalities and lifestyles is highlighted by their ages. They live for different reasons (Holden is an idealist; Spencer is a realist) and view life through very different lenses. In an ironical sense, Holden resents Spencer for doing what Holden wishes to do with others: he holds him responsible for his actions and exposes his weaknesses. Spencer puts Holden through the agony of listening to his history exam answers. But the teacher is only trying to help, and Holden recognizes this fact. It is at this point that Holden realizes how radically different he is from Mr. Spencer.

CHAPTER 3

Summary

Holden opens the chapter by stating that he is "the most terrific liar you ever saw in your life. It's awful." He talks about a wealthy alumnus of Pencey School named Ossenburger who made his fortune in the undertaking business. When he donated a large sum of money to the school, he appeared on campus and was treated like royalty. Holden found this hypocritical and refs to him as a phony: "I can just see the big phony bastard shifting into first gear and asking Jesus to send him a few more stiffs." His reason for talking about Ossenburger is that the wing of his dorm was named after the man.

Holden proceeds to list the books he enjoys reading (mysteries, classical novels, war books, etc.) and mentions his fondness for the works of his brother D.B. and of Ring Lardner. He is presently reading *Out of Africa* by Isak Dinesen. But before he can say much about that book, he is intruded upon by Robert Ackley, the boy who lives in the dorm room next to Holden. Ackley is round-shouldered, has pimples and bad teeth, and is fundamentally nasty. Holden does not like him. Ackley enters the room, picks up many of Holden's personal objects, walks around and tries to initiate a conversation in which Holden is not interested. They talk briefly about a variety of subjects: Holden's red hat (which he purchased that morning in New York), Ackley's teeth and fingernails and Holden's roommate Ward Stradlater (whom Ackley despises). Holden calls him "Ackley kid" because he knows this annoys him. Then Stradlater comes in and asks permission to wear Holden's hound's-tooth jacket. Holden consents.

Commentary

This chapter offers further examples of "phonies." Holden dislikes phoniness whenever he sees it, and seizes the occasion to mock Ossenburger the undertaker for being money-hungry. He also finds his roommate a bit phony when the latter greets Ackley, someone whom he knows does not like him. Yet his sarcasm is not bitter, it is instant and amusing. Holden has a knack for going right to the truth of a matter. He hits the jugular and then moves onto his next target. He does not dwell on a subject, but rather exposes it for what it is.

In his efforts to be truthful with us, he admits to being a liar. Though this may seem contradictory, it is more a statement about how he views society. He knows that people wear a social façade in their everyday dealings and that they rarely say what they are thinking. So in a sense, he confesses to being something of a phony himself, though in a harmless way. He is anxious to create a world for himself in which the artificial mask is discarded and in which a truthful interchange can exist between human beings. While this has deep philosophical and ethical

21

repercussions, Holden's perspective on the subject remains humorous. It would not be accurate to call him superficial since his insights are indeed profound. But since they are presented in a colloquial teenage dialect — and Salinger is brilliant at capturing this — Holden's comments often seem less serious than they actually are. He is amazingly lucid for someone in a psychiatric hospital, but then this raises the issue of society's image of the psychological requirements for being admitted to an institution. People often judge such hospital 'inmates' as being mentally incompetent or psychologically inferior, yet it is not uncommon to find that such patients are exceedingly bright, very in-tune with their emotions, and troubled more by what they see around them than by what is happening inside their own minds. Holden must not be judged as a stereotypical mental patient. His importance to society is great since he is able to point out some of mankind's most obvious deficiencies.

Holden's comic effect often comes from his penchant for exaggeration. For example, when he describes the time when Ossenburger gave a speech in the chapel, he says: "He made a speech that lasted about ten hours. He started off with about fifty corny jokes, just to show us what a regular guy he was. Very big deal." In this tone of disgust, which we find amusing, Holden debunks many of the authority figures which exist in every generation.

Salinger's technique here is almost that of stream-of-consciousness (i.e. one idea flowing directly into another without apparent organization or logic). However, it is not the kind of stream-of-consciousness which one finds in Proust, Woolf, or Joyce. Holden's speech is more accurately described as a series of narrations which lead logically from one to the next: one thing reminds Holden of another, or he finds it necessary to explain the background of something before continuing with his story. Holden is continually digressing.

CHAPTER 4

Summary

Holden follows his roommate to the washroom and talks with him as the latter shaves. Stradlater asks him to write a composition for him for his English course. Holden admits to himself that his roommate has a good body build, but he resents the fact that people who are good-looking often conclude that the world is anxious to wait on them hand-and-foot.

Stradlater tells him that his date for the evening is Jane Gallagher, a girl whom Holden knows and likes very much. Holden's relationship with her has been innocent and pure. They played checkers with one another two summers earlier when she "practically lived next door" to him. He asks Stradlater to say hello to her for him since he does not have the courage to speak to her himself.

Stradlater puts on Holden's hound's-tooth jacket for his date. In spite of himself, Holden becomes nervous and fidgets with his hat. He is protective of Jane Gallagher and does not want his roommate to take advantage of her: "I sat there for about a half hour after he left. . . I kept thinking about Jane, and about Stradlater having a date with her and all. It made me so nervous I nearly went crazy." Ackley barges in again, but this time Holden is glad to see him since it takes his mind off his anxieties.

Commentary

Holden is a sensitive, caring individual who shows concern for the well-being of Jane Gallagher, a girl he knew two summers ago. His roommate is a sexually attractive, virile young man who is careless, somewhat thoughtless and not interested in details. Stradlater spends most of his life in front of the mirror and pays little attention to anything important.

In this chapter, we see that Holden can be quite objective and truthful about himself. He is quick to announce that he is nervous by nature, and that he fidgets restlessly when nervousness troubles him. He makes no attempt to justify his nervousness or to blame others for it.

The relationship between Holden and Stradlater is based in part on mutual need. Stradlater is physically handsome and Holden admires his masculine sexuality. Holden, on the other hand, is a capable writer and can provide a useful service to his roommate. Moreover, Holden owns clothing which Stradlater borrows, and so on. In a variety of ways, the two interact well, even though Holden is essentially jealous of his colleague's lifestyle.

It is important to note at this point that Jane Gallagher represents a symbol of purity in the eyes of Holden. He is not happy about the idea that his roommate, a sexually magnetic and active young man, has ended up with Jane as a date. He does not wish to see her hurt, nor does he wish to have Stradlater take advantage of her. This situation will figure significantly in the upcoming chapters.

CHAPTER 5

Summary

Holden eats dinner in the dorm on Saturday night, bemoaning the fact that they always serve steak. He explains that the school does this so that students will tell their parents on Sunday that they had steak to eat on Saturday: "What a racket. You should've seen the steaks. They were these little hard, dry jobs that you could hardly even cut."

After dinner, Holden and a friend from the wrestling team, Mal Brossard, decide to go into Agerstown to see a movie. Holden invites Ackley to accompany them. The only movie playing was one that Brossard and Ackley had already seen. So they eat some hamburgers, play pinball and return to Pencey. Ackley goes back to Holden's room with him and lies down on his bed, picking his pimples and talking about a sexual relationship he apparently had the summer before. Holden knows that the story is pure fiction since each time Ackley tells it, the details are changed and the story comes out differently.

When Ackley finally leaves, Holden begins writing the composition for Stradlater. He writes about his dead brother Allie's left-handed baseball mitt on which his brother had written poetry. Allie died of leukemia on July 18, 1946 and it is clear that Holden misses him very much: "You'd have liked him. He was two years younger than I was, but he was about fifty times as intelligent. He was terrifically intelligent. His teachers were always writing letters to my mother, telling her what a pleasure it was having a boy like Allie in their class. . . . God he was a nice kid." He recalls how Allie used to laugh so hard he would almost fall out of his chair. The night Allie died, Holden slept in the garage and broke all the windows with his fist. His parents were going to have him psychoanalyzed and he doesn't blame them.

Holden finishes the story by ten-thirty. He is not tired so he looks out the window. He hears Ackley's snores coming from the next room and decides one has to feel sorry for people like Ackley.

Commentary

In the last chapter, we see the beginnings of a conflict which will re-occur throughout the story — namely, Holden's feelings about Jane Gallagher. In this chapter, we also discover Holden's deep feelings about his dead brother. When Allie died, Holden smashed out a number of glass windows "just for the hell of it." His anger and rage were translated through this physical action, but he was unable to identify his true feelings. Rarely is anything so violent done "just for the hell of it." Rather, there is a motivating force which propels one into action. We can understand in part why Holden has had problems at school. There are very deep emotions at war in his psyche and he has not found a suitable way to express them. It is touching that he is able to feel some form of friendship toward Ackley, despite having already confessed that he "wasn't too crazy about him, to tell . . . the truth." But this does not prevent Holden from inviting Ackley to accompany them to town.

Holden decides to write the composition for Stradlater for different reasons: he has nothing to do and is bored, and he wishes to comply with Stradlater's need to hand in a respectable paper to the English professor. Holden is a generous person, and this is shown more through his actions than his words: "I had to use Stradlater's lousy typewriter, and it kept jamming on me. The reason I didn't use my own was because I'd lent it to a guy down the hall."

The first hint of his psychoanalysis occurs when he tells how his parents considered having him examined after the violent burst of window-breaking. Again, Holden is quite objective and matter-of-fact in his narration of this.

CHAPTER 6

Summary

Holden tries to think back to the night when he heard Stradlater coming home from his date with Jane. The tension was enormous since he was worried about what may have transpired between them: "If you knew Stradlater, you'd have been worried, too. I'd double-dated with that bastard a couple of times, and I know what I'm talking about. He was unscrupulous. He really was." Holden feels hostile toward Stradlater when the latter enters the room, and this is intensified when Stradlater complains about the subject of the composition (baseball mitt): "No wonder you're flunking the hell out of here. . . You don't do one damn thing the way you're supposed to." Holden grabs the essay and rips it to shreads. He feels deep hatred for Stradlater, mostly because his roommate is a potential threat to his relationship with Jane and because he does not wish Jane to be hurt.

Stradlater has removed all of his clothes except his shorts. He approaches Holden's bed and takes playful jabs at his shoulder, claiming that he and Jane spent the evening in a car. When Holden tries to find out whether the two had sex, Stradlater replies that it is a "professional secret." This enrages Holden, who then punches him in the face. The next thing he knows, Stradlater has him on the floor and is sitting on his chest, demanding to know what is the matter. Stradlater is red in the face and furious; he does not like being taunted by his roommate, who calls him a moron. Stradlater lets Holden get up off the floor, but when Holden yells further insults at him ("You're a dirty stupid sonuvabitch of a moron"), he slams Holden with a punch that sends him back to the floor. Stradlater leaves the room and Holden looks at his bleeding face in the mirror: "It partly scared me and it partly fascinated me." The blood makes him feel tough. Then Holden goes next door to see Ackley.

Commentary

This is a tense chapter in which we realize the extent of Holden's feelings for Jane. They are not yet articulated, but there is no question about his concern for her well-being. He is angry at his roommate for telling him nothing about the girl, and this is the anger which leads ultimately to the fight between them.

Stradlater's rejection of the English composition provokes Holden and he flies into a rage. His feelings about his dead brother are intense, and the subject of Allie's baseball mitt is intricately related to Allie's personality. When Stradlater boldly complains about Holden's essay, Holden has no choice but to confiscate the composition and prevent Stradlater from using it.

In a sense, he must defend the honor of his brother and, in an indirect way, defend that of Jane Gallagher. It is not so much Stradlater that Holden despises; rather, it is what Stradlater represents: limited mentality, insensitivity toward other people's feelings, self-infatuation and so on. The physical fight is no more than the outward expression of what Holden feels inside. Though he loses the fight, he is somehow proud of having dared to assert himself.

CHAPTER 7

Summary

Holden goes into Ackley's room and begins talking with him, even though he has little respect for the neighboring student: "He was even more stupid that Stradlater." Ackley is reluctant to let Holden sleep in the vacant bed, and this infuriates Holden. He is suddenly filled with loneliness and wishes he were dead. He lies down on the bed and thinks about Jane: "It just drove me stark staring mad when I thought about her and Stradlater parked somewhere in that fat-assed Ed Banky's car."

Holden hears Stradlater return to the next room and feels profoundly lonely. He awakens Ackley from his sleep in order to ask him how one joins a monastery. He leaves Ackley's room and decides to depart immediately from Pencey: "It made me too sad and lonely." He packs his belongings and is saddened by the fact that he may disappoint his parents by being expelled from the school. His mother has just sent him a new pair of skates and it further depresses him to now turn around and pack them up again. He decides to spend a couple of days in a New York hotel in order to relax and to give his parents time to digest the schoolmaster's letter informing them of their son's expulsion from Pencey.

When his bags are packed, he walks down the corridor, turns around, and yells at the top of his lungs: "Sleep tight, ya morons!" Then he leaves rapidly, nearly falling on some peanut shells in the stairway.

Commentary

This chapter is necessary in order to make a transition between the time when Holden is a student at Pencey and the time which follows that experience. He is shown to be in a highly charged emotional state. His feelings range from concern over Jane's well-being and fears that Stradlater may have taken advantage of her; loneliness, since he feels he is without friends or allies; resentment toward his fellow students for being insensitive and unintelligent and general worries about the future. The full extent of his emotion can be appreciated in the last paragraph of the chapter: "When I had my bags and all, I stood for a while next to the stairs and took a last look down the goddam corridor. I was sort of crying. I don't know why." Clearly Holden has problems identifying with other human beings. He is extremely intelligent and has insights into life which others lack. His mind is a probing, analytical one which is at the same time highly emotional. This explains some of his conflicts. He wants the companionship and love of others, yet he finds them substandard in their living habits. Their very humanity is what disturbs him. He would prefer people whose flaws have been eliminated or, at least, tamed. The fact that he does not know, in this chapter, why he is sad is significant. We can now proceed to find out what is troubling Holden and discover how he sets about dealing with his problems.

CHAPTER 8

Summary
Holden walks all the way from the school to the train station. At Trenton, a lady gets on the train and sits down beside him, even though the car is practically empty. It amazes Holden that she places her bag right in the middle of the aisle, where everyone can trip over it.

The lady's name is Mrs. Morrow and her son Ernest attends Pencey. She asks Holden his name so that she can tell her son that they've spoken, and he replies: Rudolf Schmidt. He does not like Ernest Morrow at all and prefers not to tell his life history to his mother, even though she is a very nice person.

She notices that Holden's nose is bleeding and he explains it as being the result of an icy snowball that hit him in the face. He makes up a number of stories about her son because he knows that mothers love to hear how important their children are. Holden is attracted to her, sexually, and invites her to have a drink with him in the club car. She wonders if he is old enough and he shows her some of his grey hairs. But she turns him down politely.

Then Mrs. Morrow inquires about the Christmas vacation at Pencey. She knows that it does not begin until Wednesday and is curious why Holden is returning home so soon. He explains that he has a tiny brain tumor, but the moment he utters this, he regrets having done so. Mrs. Morrow gets off the train in Newark.

Commentary

Holden's sensitivity toward his health is underlined at the beginning of this chapter when he lists the effect of the cold on his body. The snow makes it difficult for him to walk to the train station, but his ears are "nice and warm" thanks to his hat. We feel sorry for him in this trying situation. He is alone on a cold night, rejected by his school, troubled about Jane Gallagher's welfare, angry at the limitation of his colleagues and has been badly injured by Stradlater in the fight. He is somewhat of a sorry sight with his bloody face and swollen lip. When Mrs. Morrow enters the train, she provides a touch of warmth and friendship, which puts Holden in a better frame of mind.

Earlier in the novel Holden refers to his habit of telling lies. Here is a good example of what he means: he changes his name so as to hide his true identity (fear of being recognized as a failure; reluctance to get involved in a long narration of his problems, etc.), and he invents a series of fictitious stories about Mrs. Morrow's son in an effort to impress the woman. He likes her and finds her charming. She represents something of a mother figure in her stable, concerned manner and warmth of attitude. Holden has said earlier in the chapter that he considers himself quite sexy. By inviting Mrs. Morrow to the bar, he is attempting to set up a social encounter which, even if peripherally, resembles a man-woman relationship. It is simple and unaffected, but does not work because she is reserved. Holden carries his lies through to the chapter's end. This way, she will never be able to identify him and the role he has played with her can be discarded as quickly as a mask.

This is a humorous and ingenious chapter which shows Salinger at his peak of comic description. The rapid strokes of his pen allow a genuine, but innocent relationship to emerge.

His description is simple and unadorned, and this causes the reader's imagination to sketch in many of the missing details. It shows Holden in a situation which most people have experienced at certain times of their lives: the need to impress, and the need to falsify or disguise the self in order to avoid embarrassment or pain. Holden's lies are mostly harmless and unthreatening. His approach is to romanticize his interactions with people so that they rise above the mundane and banal. He loathes that which is common and dull, opting rather for a playful, provocative point of view.

CHAPTER 9

Summary

When he arrives at Penn Station, Holden decides to place some telephone calls but cannot think of anyone to call. He thinks of calling a girl named Sally Hayes. She has written him, a "long, phony letter, inviting me over to help her trim the Christmas tree Christmas Eve and all — but I was afraid her mother'd answer the phone. Her mother knew my mother, and I could picture her breaking a goddam leg to get to the phone and tell my mother I was in New York." Mrs. Hayes had once told Sally that Holden was "wild" and that he had no direction in life. He ends up not calling anyone.

He gets into a taxi and, by mistake, gives the driver his parent's address. He tells the man to turn around once they get out of Central Park and to drive away from the East Side, where he fears seeing some of his acquaintances. Holden instructs him to go to the Edmont Hotel, where he checks in, not knowing that "the goddam hotel was full of perverts and morons."

Holden admits that he is "probably the biggest sex maniac you ever saw" and he describes the goings-on which he sees from his hotel-room window. Right across the way, he watches a man dressed in women's clothing and, in the room above this, he sees a man and woman squirting water out of their mouths at each other. He finds these activities perverted, but knows that he enjoys doing "crumby stuff" at times himself.

He toys with the idea of calling Jane Gallagher, but he decides not to do so. He calls a girl named Faith Cavendish, whose name and address had been given to him by someone at a party. She is annoyed by his call since it is so late, but when she discovers that he received her name from a guy at Princeton, she changes her tone. But she refuses to have a cocktail with him and the call ends rather unproductively.

Commentary

Holden Caulfield is now on his own, in the middle of the adult world, and is intensely aware of his aloneness. He wants to call Jane Gallagher because she represents an image of warmth, emotion and belonging, even though the two have never been formally linked to one another. But he finds himself in a dingy, seamy hotel room and is unable to justify a telephone call to the woman of his dreams. Jane is reminiscent of *Don Quixote's* Dulcinea: she is almost certainly unaware of Holden's affection for her, yet she is extremely important to his emotional well-being.

Faith Cavendish is several notches lower than Jane in Holden's esteem, but he resorts to her in an effort to fill the void. Sexual matters confuse him since he can never figure out his feelings: "Sex is something I really don't understand too hot. You never know *where* the hell you are. I keep making up these sex rules for myself, and then I break them right away."

When Faith suggests that they have cocktails the next day instead of that very evening, Holden says he cannot make it, that they must meet right then. This is an example of his inability to read the situation correctly — or at least his inexperience with human negotiation. He has had numerous encounters with girls, yet he fails to obtain the desired results with Faith. This is due to his haste, the time of night, his lack of familiarity with her, and any number of other reasons. Holden knows that he did not handle himself correctly: "I really fouled that up." So he resolves to spend the evening alone. His aloneness gives him the occasion to focus on his thoughts and lead us closer to the dénouement of his story.

CHAPTER 10

Summary

Holden wants to call his sister Phoebe, but cannot take the chance of having his parents answer the phone. Holden likes Phoebe because she is sensible, even though she is only ten years old. She is smart and this impresses him: "I mean if you tell old

Phoebe something, she knows exactly what the hell you're talking about." But he thinks she is a bit too affectionate.

He changes his shirt and goes downstairs to the Lavender Room, the hotel night club. There is no one his age in the bar and he is seated at the back table. There are three women at the next table and Holden begins making eyes at them. He thinks they are rather ugly, but takes an interest in the blonde, who gets up and dances with him.

She turns out to be an excellent dancer but pays no attention to Holden's attempts to make conversation. He thinks she is a moron, but accompanies her to her table. He tells the three of them that his name is Jim Steele and has problems getting a conversation going: "And the whole three of them kept looking all around the goddam room, like as if they expected a flock of goddam *movie stars* to come in any minute." The two ugly ones, named Marty and Laverne, he thinks are sisters; the blonde, Bernice, works with them in an insurance office in Seattle, Washington.

Holden dances with all three of them. Laverne is not bad as a dancer, but Marty is impossible: "Old Marty was like dragging the Statue of Liberty around the floor." He buys them each two drinks, and when they finish them, they stand up abruptly to leave. It depresses Holden that the women intend to get up early for the first show at Radio City Music Hall: "If somebody, some girl in an awful-looking hat, for instance, comes all the way to New York — from Seattle, Washington, for God's sake — and ends up getting up early in the morning to see the goddam first show at Radio City Music Hall, it makes me so depressed I can't stand it. I'd've bought the whole three of them a *hundred* drinks if only they hadn't told me that."

Commentary

What hits Holden more clearly than anything in this chapter is the sense of not fitting in and of feeling lonely. He wants to speak with his sister Phoebe because she makes sense, despite her young age, and because she is interesting. He attempts to enjoy himself with the three women in the bar, but they are more interested in finding "movie stars" than in conversing with a minor. The waiter refuses to serve him liquor, and this reinforces Holden's sense of not belonging in the outside world. Internally, he understands human psychology, but externally he is unable to make things work for himself. This rejection produces depression, which will set things in motion for an obsessive search for happiness, for meaning, for truth and sincerity. Phony people stand no chance in Holden Caulfield's world.

CHAPTER 11

Summary

On his way out to the lobby, Holden begins thinking of Jane Gallagher again. He describes the way in which they met: Jane's dog disturbed Holden's mother, who called Jane's mother with her complaints. Then, a few days later, Holden saw Jane at the club swimming pool and began talking with her. After that, they became good friends and spent a lot of time together, though there was never a physical relationship.

Holden recalls Jane's appearance and describes her mouth, which always remains slightly open. He is in love with her and thinks she is pretty, even though his mother disagrees. One afternoon, he came close to kissing her. They were playing checkers on her screened-in porch and Mr. Cudahy, the drunken "booze hound" married to Jane's mother, came out onto the porch looking for cigarettes. He asked Jane twice where he could find some, but she ignored him. When he left, Jane began crying and Holden moved over to sit beside her. He kissed her all over her face, but she would not let him near her mouth. Holden still does not understand what was bothering her that day.

They used to go to the movies together and would hold hands. One day, Jane put her hand on the back of Holden's neck, and this is what Holden thinks about as he sits in the hotel lobby. It drives him crazy to think that she was with Stradlater in Ed Banky's car.

He gets in a cab and goes to Ernie's, a night club in Greenwich Village.

Commentary

The evening spent in the Lavender Room had not been satisfying for Holden. He was in search of companionship, but found only three dull women. He wanted an alcoholic drink, but the waiter would not serve him. He thought about Jane

Gallagher, and became angry at the thought of Stradlater being with her, and so on. Nostalgia and memories of Jane are pleasant for him, but they always lead to the conclusion that nothing ever happened between the two of them. In order to flee this atmosphere of depression and loneliness, he goes to a Greenwich Village bar.

Ernie, the man who runs the bar, is a terrific snob and "won't hardly even talk to you unless you're a big shot or a celebrity." Holden realizes that people are often judged by their status in life, whether this be in terms of money, age, profession, or some other category. He does not find that people want to be with him, or that he wants to be with them. Despite his need to feel loved, he cannot get beyond the idea that people are phony, insincere, and less intelligent than they ought to be.

Jane is portrayed as a sensitive, vulnerable girl with deep emotional feelings. She is not "an icicle" and is far from being a bore: she reads intensely, sees lots of movies, and Holden finds her stimulating, as well as beautiful. She is somewhat of an ideal woman for him in that she is apparently unobtainable, yet very much the object of his desires. Part of Holden's quest for meaning will revolve around his attempts to find satisfaction in his relationship with Jane.

CHAPTER 12

Summary

The cab driver who takes Holden to "Ernie's" is named Horwitz and is friendlier with Holden than the last cab driver. But he finds Holden's question about the ducks in Central Park annoying: Holden wants to know where the ducks go in the winter, but nobody can answer his question. Even Horwitz becomes grouchy about it. Holden revises his opinion about the man and finds that he is no fun. When he asks the cab driver to join him for a drink, Horwitz turns him down: "I ain't got no time for no liquor, bud. . . How the hell old are you, anyways? Why ain'tcha home in bed?"

Ernie's is crowded with prep school and college students. Holden is scornful of Ernie: when Ernie plays the piano, everyone treats it as if it were a sacred rite, a holy occasion. Holden believes that nobody is *that* good and he dislikes the pomp surrounding Ernie's performances.

The audience goes wild over Ernie. Ernie turns around and gives what Holden calls a "phony, *humble* bow." Holden believes that people always clap for the wrong things and this depresses him: "I damn near got my coat back and went back to the hotel, but it was too early and I didn't feel much like being all alone."

Holden gets seated at a table against the wall, behind a post where he couldn't see anything. The waiter serves him alcohol, paying no attention to his age: "If you were only around six years old, you could get liquor at Ernie's. . . You could even be a dope fiend and nobody'd care."

At one table next to him, a dopey-looking guy is relating the events of a pro football game to an ugly girl. At another table, there is a "Joe Yale-looking guy in a gray flannel suit" talking to a "terrific looking girl." The man is telling her about someone in his dorm who ate a bottle of aspirins and nearly died — but all the while he tells her this, he is touching her under the table.

Suddenly, a girl whom Holden's brother D.B. had dated comes up to him. She is Lillian Simmons and Holden thinks she is a phony. She introduces Holden to the navy man with her ("His name was Commander Blop or something") and blocks the aisle so that no one can pass. She tells Holden that he is "getting handsomer by the minute" and invites him to join them at their table. Holden replies that he was just on his way out, and this angers her: "Well, you little so-and-so. All right for you. Tell your big brother I hate him."

Holden leaves, even though he would like to hear Ernie play something "halfway decent." He is angry that people are always ruining things.

Commentary

Holden's insight into human beings is extraordinary. He understands basic human motives and sees through all the play-acting that is part of social interaction. He knows that people are essentially hypocritical, but decides that "if you want to stay alive, you have to say that stuff."

Again, we see how lonely and isolated he is. It is not comforting for him to see Lillian Simmons, even if she is someone he recognizes. He is searching for true meaning, not superficial chit-chat, and he has no time for people whose imposition on his time amounts to nothing positive or of interest. At one point in the chapter, he states his desire to go home and talk with his sister. There is no question that he feels out of place, especially in the cold, unwelcoming world of a New York night-club. His age is a factor here since he knows that most people in these clubs are older than he, but his sophistication is such that he manipulates his way around most obstacles.

Perhaps more important than anything else in this chapter is Holden's scorn for people. He takes a dislike to Horwitz the cab-driver, to Ernie the piano-player, to Lillian Simmons and her boyfriend and to the people at tables beside his own in the bar. Holden despises their insincerity and cannot understand how they can be happy in such a limited lifestyle. To him, they appear to be living a lie and have no fundamental meaning to their lives. It is as if he has been reincarnated into a historical period for which he has little or no preparation. His tolerance for their actions is almost non-existent.

Yet Holden is not despicable or unlikeable. On the contrary, he strikes an amusing, magnetic picture in his fuss and fume about the phonies. Much of his negativity is a mask for other feelings, notably his depression and the isolation associated with that depression. Most people who are depressed experience loneliness, isolation, a feeling of being severed from humanity. Many are contemptuous of other people's actions, and often those who criticize the most heavily are the ones who feel most vulnerable within their own personality. When we consider Holden from this point of view, his words and actions make more sense to us: he is lonely, sad, troubled about his position in society, and unsure of what lies ahead. Holden's concern about the ducks in Central Park is also important. He asks Horwitz what happens to them in the wintertime: ". . . does somebody come around in a truck or something and take them away, or do they fly away by themselves — go south or something?" In the novel, we shall see that Holden takes upon himself the burden of protecting, or watching out for, little children. His concern extends to other vulnerable creatures — such as ducks.

CHAPTER 13

Summary
Holden walks forty-one blocks back to his hotel. He regrets

having had his gloves stolen at Pencey since it is bitterly cold outside. His lost gloves provide a subject he can use to describe his essential cowardice when it comes to confronting people: if he knew who had stolen his gloves, he would not have challenged the person to a fight, but would probably have backed down. Being tough on the outside is one thing, but showing this toughness to someone else is not part of Holden's nature.

Thinking about his "yellowness" insofar as fighting is concerned depresses him, so he decides to stop for a drink. But he changes his mind when a drunken Cuban breathes in his face while asking for street directions.

He returns to his hotel and is asked by the elevator man whether he wishes to hire a prostitute. Holden accepts the proposition and quickly enters his room in order to fix himself up. He is nervous and admits to being a virgin. He claims to have had numerous opportunities for sex, but always stopped when the girl he was with asked him to stop. He thinks that a prostitute will help him perfect his style in case he ever gets married.

The prostitute arrives. She is blonde and not too friendly. When she pulls her dress over her head, Holden feels peculiar and is not sure what to do: "Sexy was about the *last* thing I was feeling. I felt much more depressed than sexy." She asks him several times if he has a watch and finally he replies no.

Holden wants to talk with her for a while before engaging in sex, but she says: "What the heck ya wanna talk about?" Finally he decides that he is in no mood for sex. He tells this to her and says he will pay her nonetheless. She is suddenly intrigued by him and sits on his lap, which makes Holden very nervous. He tells her that he just had a serious operation on his "clavichord" and is unable to have sex with her. Angered, she gets dressed and leaves.

Commentary

Though on the surface this chapter seems merely a continuation of the others, it is in fact an important one in our understanding of Holden Caulfield. To begin with, Holden is a virgin and we can see that much of his carousing, and much of his frank conversation, has been a façade for his inexperience. He has not boasted openly of having had sex, but has implied often that he knows the ropes. His confession of virginity opens up a new channel in the communication between narrator and reader/analyst: we feel much closer to him and more sympathetic toward his present situation.

Holden is in search of deep meaning in life. He desires truth, warmth, support and understanding from those around him. He is highly intelligent and can see through the falseness of human dialogue. But he is also capable of engaging in this very falseness by putting on airs when he is with other people. His façade is a defense mechanism against getting hurt and he is quick to admit the truth about himself. Therefore, we must overlook his tendency to fictionalize his life (e.g. using the name Jim Steele; lying about his age, and so on) and realize that these are superficial attempts to fit in with people whom he judges to be superficial.

But the real importance of this chapter lies in the contrast it offers to Holden's search for meaning. While he wants desperately to find love with a woman, he is revolted by the prostitute and cannot function with her. The prostitute has had experience with sex and Holden has not; she is cold even though he attempts to be friendly; he wishes to talk with her but she is not interested; he wants to take his time before having sex but she wants to get it over with rapidly. Though he narrates his story in a 'cool,' collected fashion, he turns out to be devastated by the impersonal tone of this encounter and becomes depressed by it. He is not the playboy type and discovers this for himself when confronted with his first sexual experience. The episode with the prostitute, then, is significant because it highlights Holden's sensitivities and shows to what extent he is vulnerable as a budding adult.

Holden has ridiculed his roommate Stradlater for being sexually adventurous, yet when the time comes for Holden to try his wings, he is unable to do so. Intellectually, Holden is superior to the prostitute, but he is still a minor when it comes to being sexually active. Or at least this is part of the message derived from the context. The writing style in this chapter — short, choppy sentences and an uneasy dialogue between the two characters — reinforces the tensions Holden feels.

Holden's search for meaning cannot be gratified by meaningless, random contacts with people who are of no importance to him. Indeed, the sordid quality of the encounter between Holden and the prostitute can be felt clearly by the reader. Holden is not in an enviable position. This chapter shows us that his rejection from Pencey and from his classmates at that school follows him to the streets and hotels of New York, where he finds himself in the same situation: people are the same wherever one goes, and personal values must be arrived at through a long, slow process.

Salinger is brilliant in his manipulation of detail. He is at once capable of drawing attention to the physical aspects of Holden's surroundings (e.g. clothing, hotel lobbies, bar-rooms) and to the inner workings of Holden's mind. The psychological detail is no less shrewd and poignant than the external descriptions of location. In both, the novelist uses short, rapid-fire sentences that give us just enough information to allow for an understanding of the context. Rarely does he use adverbs or strings of adjectives. Salinger favors strong verbs and nouns in his attempt to portray a bold, immediate confrontation with reality. The style is in part impressionistic (insofar as it creates impressions in our minds) and realistic. It is never obscure or rambling, but always pointed and focused on the subject at hand.

CHAPTER 14

Summary

When the prostitute leaves, Holden sits in a chair for a while and smokes several cigarettes. It is becoming light outside and Holden feels miserable. He resorts to talking out loud to his brother Allie, something he does when he is depressed.

He gets into bed and feels like praying, but admits to being somewhat of an atheist. He likes Jesus but finds the "other stuff in the Bible" annoying. And he thinks that ministers are phony with their "Holy Joe" voices.

As he lies there smoking a cigarette, someone knocks at his door. It is Maurice, the elevator operator and the prostitute, demanding five more dollars for her 'services.' Holden has fulfilled the terms of their agreement by paying her five dollars, but the two are in cahoots with one another and insist on more money. Maurice gives Holden a push and enters the room, even though Holden is still in his pajamas.

The man threatens Holden, who refuses to pay. Holden is extremely nervous and his voice shakes uncontrollably. The prostitute grabs the money from Holden's wallet and Holden begins to cry. The man refuses to back off, even though the prostitute suggests they leave. Holden screams insults at him, which angers the man further. He punches Holden in the stomach and he and the prostitute leave.

Holden stays on the floor for a moment and thinks he is dying. Getting up, he walks to the bathroom and imagines that he has been shot, that he will get dressed and exit from the room with his pistol, go downstairs and shoot Maurice the elevator man. He would then return to his room, call up Jane Gallagher, and have her come over to bandage his wounds. But he concludes that this is an effect that one finds only in Hollywood movies: "The goddam movies. They can ruin you."

He takes a bath, goes to bed, and falls asleep after an hour, even though he feels like committing suicide.

Commentary

Holden pays dearly for the price of having a prostitute in his room. She is ruthless and is prepared to take advantage of Holden's naïveté. Maurice, the elevator man, is a phony and treats Holden brutally in order to extract five extra dollars from him. Recall that this novel was published in 1951 when five dollars were worth considerably more than they are today. But the point remains the same: life in society is a brutal, savage process for those unequipped to fight back.

This chapter underlines Holden's vulnerability and lack of experience with the sordid side of life. Though he is from New York, he has lived a protected existence in the world of the Upper East Side and in boarding school. This is his first independent contact with the down-and-out side of Manhattan and, in a broader sense, with the world of phonies whom he so bitterly despises.

Injustice is presented as the consequence of getting involved with shady characters, with seamy individuals. It is a lesson which all picaresque heroes are taught and it moves Holden one step closer to his declaration of hatred for society. The underworld of Manhattan is a long way from the protected environment of his family.

The message of this chapter is: the idealized world of sex and glamour belongs strictly in the Hollywood movies. Injustice and corruption run rampant and innocent people are often hurt.

CHAPTER 15

Summary

It is ten o'clock when Holden awakens. He telephones Sally Hayes, whom he has known for a long time but whom he considers a phony. He makes a date with her to see a play that afternoon.

He leaves the hotel and gets in a cab, but doesn't know where to go. It is only Sunday and he cannot go home until Wednesday. He goes to Grand Central Station and checks his bags into a strong box. He counts his money and sees that he is not exactly rich, but he reveals that his father is quite wealthy. Mr. Caulfield is a corporate lawyer.

Holden eats breakfast in a little sandwich bar. Two nuns enter and sit next to him, whereupon he strikes up a conversation with them. One of them has a very kind face and Holden makes a ten-dollar contribution to their cause. They are schoolteachers from Chicago who are in New York to begin teaching at a convent school: one teaches history and the other English. Holden wonders what nuns think about when they read books with sexy characters in them.

Holden tells the English teacher about the books they studied in English this semester. When he mentions *Romeo and Juliet*, she stops him enthusiastically and asks him a question about it: "It was sort of embarrassing, in a way, to be talking about *Romeo and Juliet* with her. I mean that play gets pretty sexy in some parts, and she was a nun and all, but she *asked* me."

The nuns prepare to leave and Holden tries to pay their check, but they insist on paying themselves. They tell Holden how sweet he is.

Holden enjoys talking with them and would like to continue the conversation but is relieved that they made no attempt to find out if he is Catholic. As they leave, he regrets not having given them more money.

Commentary

The nuns represent a bright spot in Holden's self-imposed exile. They are pure, honest and symbolic of a virtuous lifestyle. Having been through a series of unsettling interactions, Holden is more than happy to engage in harmless chit-chat with them. This chapter comes as a sort of 'breather' in the ever-mounting tension of Holden's existence. He admits, indirectly, in the first part of the chapter that he is directionless: "I got a cab outside the hotel, but I didn't have the faintest damn idea where I was going.'' While this refers specifically to his momentary confusion about where to go in the city, it also represents on a larger scale his disorientation in society, in life.

Holden is now slightly more prepared for his date with Sally Hayes. He has eaten a hearty breakfast, has spent time with two stable women of the church and has made a charitable contribution to their institution. Psychologically, he is in a better frame of mind than the night before as he has been positively affected by the nuns. Now he is ready for his next experience.

CHAPTER 16

Summary

Holden still has two hours before his meeting with Sally, so he sets out on a long walk. He goes in the direction of Broadway since he wants to buy a record for his sister Phoebe. On his way, he walks behind a family of three who have just been to church. Holden likes them and attempts to hear what the young boy is humming. The child is singing "If a body catch a body coming through the rye," and this makes Holden feel better: "It made me feel not so depressed any more."

Broadway is crowded with people swarming all over the place in their Sunday clothes, determined to go to the movies. Holden despises this desire in them. But he becomes happy once again when he discovers the record for Phoebe in the first store he enters.

He decides to telephone Jane but hangs up when the girl's mother answers. Then he goes looking for theater tickets and chooses orchestra seats for *I Know My Love*, starring the Lunts. He feels that Sally will like that kind of show, even though he has no use for it. In fact, he hates actors: "They never act like people. They just think they do." He finds them phony.

He goes to Central Park but is depressed because everything is gloomy: rain on the park benches, cold weather, soggy cigar butts, etc. He asks a girl if she knows where Phoebe Caulfield is, but the girl is of no help. He walks all the way over to the Museum of Natural History in an attempt to find her and, as he does, he reminisces about the marvelous moments when he used to see the museum exhibits with his classmates. He realizes that every time he saw the exhibits, he was a different person, even though the exhibits never changed.

Having walked all the way through the park to the museum, Holden decides not to go inside as he feels Phoebe is not there. So he takes a cab back to the Biltmore Hotel where he is to meet Sally. He does not want to see her, but he has made a commitment and intends to honor it.

Commentary

Holden notices that life goes on around him even if he would like things to remain the same. He is nostalgic about the times when, as a child, he went to the Museum with his class, year after year, and nothing ever changed there. The Indians were always standing in the same spot and the canoes were always filled with the same men. This resistance to change is something that characterizes Holden's reluctance to give up his past and move into the future. He feels threatened by the future's uncertainty and prefers the calmness of known events.

The nuns from Chapter 15 have put him in a more optimistic frame of mind. There is the suggestion of divine intervention at the moment when man is at his lowest point, down-and-out and depressed. Holden surfaces from his interaction with the nuns as a more positive, happier person. But this happiness is short-lived because he is immediately thrown into contact with the sordid reality of life: Broadway, Central Park, and hordes of uncaring human beings who pay no attention to him.

His sister Phoebe represents a glimmer of hope on an otherwise hostile horizon. Like Jane Gallagher, she is pure, honest and virtuous. There is some tension involved in the idea that Holden is so close to his home, yet so far away. Central Park is only moments from his family's residence on Seventy-first Street, but Holden must travel like a vagabond until the time is right for his return home. His mother is nervous and Holden does not wish to upset her prematurely with the news of his expulsion from Pencey. So he must wait. And this period of waiting creates tension and suspense.

Holden's comments about his environment often have more than one meaning, as we saw in the case where he entered a taxi but didn't know where to go. The literal meaning is self-evident, while the symbolic meaning refers to his position in life, to his role in the universe. Such is the case in this chapter when Holden says: "It didn't seem at all like Christmas was coming soon. It didn't seem like *anything* was coming." He is gloomy about the future and this is the more significant mode of interpretation for such statements.

On the bright side, however, Holden finds gratification in simple things, such as children who thank him for being kind and helping them. More than once we have seen Holden's sensitivity and fundamental goodness of character. If he is pessimistic or negative about life, it is largely due to his feeling that human sensitivity is snuffed out by the phoniness of adult living with its corruption and vulgarity. The basic values which he holds dear are often lost by people in their scramble for honor, glory, wealth, and personal satisfaction — and this depresses Holden.

We have in this chapter the first reference to the meaning of the novel's title, *Catcher in the Rye*. As Holden is walking down Broadway, he notices the filth and sleaziness everywhere around him. He is uncomfortable in this environment and decides to leave as soon as he finds the record for Phoebe. But as he moves down the sidewalk, he falls behind a family of three who have just been to church. The little boy is singing to himself a verse which makes Holden very happy: "If a body catch a body coming through the rỳe." This is part of a poem by Robert Burns; the correct line is actually: "If a body *meet* a body coming through the rye."

The line is significant although the implications of it are not made clear until a later chapter. Recall that Holden narrates this story from a mental hospital. He has had a nervous breakdown and is sufficiently recovered to tell his tale. Society is an environment in which he has found enormous corruption and vulgarity, much harm and havoc. He knows that the children of the world are ruined by the corruption of adults around them and, as he states later in the novel, his new purpose in life will be to help save the children from this vulgarity. He knows that the world will always have evil and crime, but he wishes to intervene whenever possible and reassert the value of goodness. His goal will be to erase evil and to help mankind as a brotherhood in its movement toward self-awareness. Human dignity is vital to Holden's existence and the only way to guarantee this on a long-term basis is to assist children in maintaining their innocence from the dangers of adulthood.

None of this is contained within this chapter. It will be revealed later on. But it is difficult to understand why Holden is made happy by the little boy's singing unless one has an idea of what the song means to Holden. The little boy is described by Holden in gentle, caring terms: "The kid was swell. He was walking in the street, instead of on the sidewalk, but right next to the curb. He was making out like he was walking a very straight line, the way kids do, and the whole time he kept singing and humming." Holden notes that the child's parents pay no attention to him.

This child represents innocence and youth unspoiled by adult vulgarity. An understanding of this point is essential in an appreciation of *Catcher in the Rye*. Holden will later reveal: "I keep picturing all these little kids in this big field of rye. . . . If they're running and they don't look where they're going, I have to come out from somewhere and catch them. That's all I'd do all day. I'd just be the catcher in the rye and all. I know it's crazy." He sees himself as the savior of children, of innocence, of basic human dignity. And while this is developed more fully toward the end of the novel, the germ for his philosophy is already present in this chapter.

CHAPTER 17

Summary

Holden goes to the clock in the Biltmore Hotel and waits for Sally. He sees a lot of school girls in the lobby and wonders if they will marry boring, mean guys. Then Sally arrives and looks terrific: "I felt like marrying her the minute I saw her. I'm crazy. I didn't even *like* her much, and yet all of a sudden I felt like I was in love with her and wanted to marry her."

They take a cab to the theater and, on the way, Holden kisses her, telling her that he loves her. Several times Holden admits to the reader/analyst that he is crazy. The play bores him, mostly because he knows it is just a bunch of actors acting. At intermission, they go out for a cigarette "with all the other jerks . . . What a deal that was. You never saw so many phonies in all your life, everybody smoking their ears off and talking about the play so that everybody could hear and know how sharp they were."

Sally sees someone she knows and this friend comes over to talk with them. Sally makes a big deal about him and Holden finds it all quite artificial. They begin name-dropping with such speed that it almost becomes a competition to see who knows the most people. The name-dropping is continued after the next intermission as well: "The worst part was, the jerk had one of those very phony, Ivy League voices, one of those very tired, snobby voices."

After the show, Sally suggests they go ice-skating at Radio City. They rent the equipment and end up being the worst skaters on the ice. So they go inside and have cokes, during which time Holden confesses his hatred for school, New York, taxicabs and everything. Sally asks him not to shout, but Holden thinks he has not been shouting.

After talking for a moment about the horrors of being a college student, Holden suggests to Sally that they take a friend's car and leave town for a couple of weeks. His plan would lead them into the woods, where they would get married, live in a cabin and chop their own wood. Holden would get a job. Sally replies: "You can't just *do* something like that." She thinks it would be better for them to do all this after Holden goes to college, but he retorts that he would be a different person at that point.

After explaining himself fully, he believes that he and Sally hate each other. He looks at Sally and says: "C'mon, let's get outa here. You give me a royal pain in the ass, if you want to know the truth." Sally hits the ceiling at his comment. Impulsively, Holden begins to laugh.

When Holden regains his composure, he realizes that Sally is not someone with whom he would have enjoyed a trip in the woods anyway, nor would he have taken her with him if she had consented: "The terrible part, though, is that I *meant* it when I asked her . . . I swear to God I'm a madman."

Commentary

This is one of the novel's longest chapters, but essentially it has two major ideas: (1) Holden dislikes phony people such as actors, theater-goers who pretend to know everything during intermissions and college students; (2) he wishes to flee this environment of artificiality and travel to some place which is pure, natural and unspoiled by civilization. It is not exactly a Rousseau-like situation where he chants the glory of nature and of uncivilized man. Rather, he prefers man to be simply what he is: emotional, intelligent, clear-minded, unaffected and decent.

Sally is no more than an instrument through which Holden can ventilate his rage about vulgarity and human deception. She represents the young adult already in the process of becoming corrupt. She values the status quo (e.g. the college education, obtaining a secure job, etc.) and has no feeling for Holden's fantasies about human purity. She is satisfied with compromise. Holden is not.

CHAPTER 18

Summary

Holden leaves the rink and enters a restaurant, where he telephones Jane. She is not in so he calls Carl Luce, an intellectual whom he met while still a student at the Whooton School. Carl agrees to meet him for a drink at ten o'clock at the Wicker Bar on 54th Street.

With time to kill, Holden goes to the movies at Radio City: "It was probably the worst thing I could've done. . . . I came in when the goddam stage show was on. The Rockettes were kicking their heads off." He resents the phoniness of the show.

The movie begins and Holden detests it. It is too contrived for his taste. The plot is so artificial that it is completely unbelievable. Holden is amazed that the lady beside him cried throughout the entire picture: "The phonier it got, the more she cried."

On his way to the Wicker Bar, Holden begins thinking about war. He does not believe he could stand to be in the army: "I'm sort of glad they've got the atomic bomb invented. If there's ever another war, I'm going to sit right the hell on top of it."

Commentary

The principle idea of this chapter is that Holden despises phoniness so much, it almost nauseates him when he's in contact with it. The discussion of war is somewhat symbolic: Holden is at war with himself and with society. He is in a fragile emotional state and when he says that he would sit on top of the atomic bomb, this suggests indirectly that he is, in fact, sitting on a bomb of his own. He senses the rage inside as he mentions how phony people cause him to "puke" and he knows that the only way to save himself is through an escape to greener pastures:

"I swear, if there's ever another war, they better just take me out and stick me in front of a firing squad. I wouldn't object." The war is, here, a psychological one, and the firing squad represents the solution to Holden's conflict: death, or psychiatric hospital, or a cabin in Vermont.

CHAPTER 19

Summary

The Wicker Bar is in the swanky Seton Hotel: "It's one of those places that are supposed to be very sophisticated and all, and the phonies are coming in the window." He arrives early, sits down at the bar, and has a couple of drinks while watching for Luce. He watches some of the homosexuals (which he calls "flits") and mentions that Luce knows every homosexual in the United States. Holden thinks Luce is "flitty" himself.

When Luce arrives, Holden asks him how his sex life is. Luce tells him to relax; he is annoyed with what he calls "typical Caulfield questions." When Holden digs for more information, Luce states that his new girlfriend is a sculptress in her 30's who lives in the Village. Holden is amazed and wonders if older women are better at sex than younger ones. Luce asks him when he is going to grow up.

Holden resents Luce for setting limits on the discussion: "These intellectual guys don't like to have an intellectual conversation with you unless they're running the whole thing."

Holden confesses that his sex life is terrible. He is not able to maintain sexual desire for a girl if he does not like her intensely. Luce concludes that Holden should see a psychoanalyst; Luce's father is an analyst. Luce is bored and shows little interest in Holden. He suggests that Holden make an appointment to see his father if he really wants to learn something about the patterns of his own mind.

When Luce gets up to leave, Holden asks him to have one more drink: "Have just one more drink. Please. I'm lonesome as hell. No kidding." But Luce refuses to stay. Holden decides that Luce is "a pain in the ass," but that he has a fine vocabulary.

Commentary

Holden's loneliness is now reaching extraordinary depths.

We can see that he is anxious about his emotions since he bombards Luce with curious, probing questions about sexuality. He realizes that he is becoming too personal, but cannot help himself: the questions reflect a desire to understand his own feelings and to relate on a deeply human level to another male of similar age.

Luce is an example of a different sort of phony: the intellectual. He has no time for anyone else's feelings, nor does he show compassion for a human being in need. There is no reason why he agreed to meet Holden at the Bar other than to have a drink, satisfy his curiosity about Holden, and perhaps to investigate the goings-on at the bar that evening. Like Sally, Luce is an instrument through which Holden views another aspect of the phony world. One by one, his contacts with people are being cut off, and the only meaningful relationships left to him are Jane (who does not answer her phone) and Phoebe (whom he cannot see before Wednesday).

CHAPTER 20

Summary

Holden sits at the bar until about one o'clock getting drunk. As he had done back in the Edmont Hotel, he goes through the motions of having a bullet in his stomach: "I kept keeping my hand under my jacket to keep the blood from dripping." Of course this is all in his imagination; he has not been shot.

He wants to call Jane, but decides not to at the last minute. Instead, he telephones Sally. She comes on the line, tells him to stop screaming and wants to know who he is with. He accepts her earlier invitation to help trim the tree on Christmas Eve and she tells him to go to bed. She hangs up on him. Holden wishes he had not phoned her: "When I'm drunk, I'm a madman."

The piano player meets Holden in the washroom and tells him to go home, but Holden can only say to him: "No home to go to. No kidding." When the man leaves, Holden begins to cry: "I don't know why, but I was [crying]. I guess it was because I was feeling so damn depressed and lonesome." The hat-check girl is friendly with him and shows concern for his health. She suggests he go home to bed and look after himself.

Holden leaves the bar and makes his way over to Central

Park. Once there, he accidentally drops Phoebe's record and it shatters into fifty pieces. He enters the park and finds it extremely dark. Although he knows every inch of the park, he cannot find the lagoon where the ducks swim.

His hair is wet from having dunked his head in cold water at the bar's washroom and he is afraid of dying from pneumonia: "I felt sorry as hell for my mother and father. Especially my mother, because she still isn't over my brother Allie yet." He hopes that when he dies, someone has the sense to dump him in a river instead of putting him in a cemetery, where all sorts of dead bodies and tombstones lie.

Holden has almost no money left, but he approaches the lagoon and skips his coins across the water. He realizes that Phoebe would be grief-stricken if he were to die, so he decides to return home, despite the consequences. He walks to his apartment house, which is close to Central Park, and prepares to talk with his sister.

Commentary

This chapter is of great importance. It is, in many ways, the turning point of the book. When Holden becomes drunk in the bar, he returns to an idea which has surfaced before, namely, his sense of death, blood and destruction. His drunken state is important because it allows him to express his thoughts without the censureship and inhibitions imposed by his superego, his conscience. We see a Holden who is totally without defenses, who has been hurt by circumstances and who experiences this hurt in a metaphorical fashion — through the imagery of a gunshot wound: "I was the only guy at the bar with a bullet in their guts. I kept putting my hand under my jacket, on my stomach and all, to keep the blood from dripping all over the place. I didn't want anybody to know I was even wounded. I was concealing the fact that I was a wounded sonuvabitch."

This quotation can be interpreted in many ways: a psychoanalyst might choose to see the deterioration of Holden's conscious mind and the breaking-off into a psychotic state, where sensations and images occur that have no grounding in 'reality'; another viewpoint might assert that Holden is merely transferring into concrete terms his emotional sensations of pain. Whatever the interpretation, one thing is certain: Holden is hurt. The French philosopher Sartre might have called it an 'existential crisis' in the sense that Holden's very existence is now at stake.

To be sure, Holden has not actually been shot, nor is he dripping with blood. But this imagery lends itself well to the idea of war, of strife, of ongoing conflict, and this describes the terrain of Holden's mind quite correctly. He is at war, has been wounded by his life experiences, and the drunken stupor leaves him vulnerable. He is very lucid about his own situation and knows that he walks a fine line between sanity and confusion. This is what prompts him to admit: "When I'm drunk, I'm a madman."

The focal point of the chapter comes when the piano player from the bar suggests that Holden go home. The boy's reply is: "No home to go to." This is true on both the literal level, since he cannot go home until Wednesday, and the figurative level, as he feels no sense of rapport with anyone, anywhere — he is like an alien from some other planet stranded on Earth without recourse to his own people.

The hat-girl at the bar is sympathetic and kind toward Holden. This is the type of person to whom he gravitates, for whom he feels warmth and support. He is very child-like, though not childish, in this regard. People who are genuine and not phony are the ones Holden Caulfield respects.

The record which he purchased for Phoebe breaks while he is in the park. This is a symbol which, like most symbols, can be viewed from several perspectives. For instance, the record represents the bond he has with his sister and with all pure, innocent people. It is the language of music, of emotion, that bonds them, not that of ambition, vulgarity and corruption. When he enters the park with wet hair, Holden fantasizes about his death and realies how shattering it would be for Phoebe if he were to die. The record is a premonition of this fantasy: by shattering, it demonstrates to Holden how fragile human relationships can be and how careful one must be to preserve them. The record is also a symbol, at this point in Holden's pilgrimage, of his own fragility: his life appears to be shattered, and the purity of harmless music (i.e. the record) is destroyed by the hardness of the ground (i.e. difficulties of living).

Holden's walk into Central Park late at night parallels, on a metaphorical level, his sinking deeper and deeper into despair. He enters a sort of twilight zone which is dark, cold and dangerous. He is alone, lonely and fearful in this world without people: "I kept walking and walking, and it kept getting darker and darker and spookier and spookier. I didn't see one person the whole time I was in the park."

But he has the shattered remains of Phoebe's record under his arm in an envelope and decides, now that he has reached the bottom, to return home. Phoebe is the one who draws him back to civilization and to life. She is the only person capable of saving Holden from the depths of his despair. She is, we might say, accessible to him; Sally is part accessible (through dating and conversations) and part inaccessible (through her commitment to phony values); Jane Gallagher is completely inaccessible to him (she is never available via the telephone; she has dated Stradlater, the enemy, etc.). The three girls represent a progression from the accessible to the inaccessible and play important roles in Holden's life based on what they represent. An illustration of their relative positions in Holden's life would look like this:

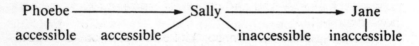

Since Holden cannot obtain Jane, and since his experiences with Sally have proved highly unsatisfactory, he has no alternative but to seek salvation through Phoebe: "I figured I'd better sneak home and see her, in case I died and all."

Holden has the will to live, and indeed he will not die. But in order to keep from succumbing to a world of phoniness and corruption, he takes refuge in innocence and youth. This will take on the important connotation, very soon, of Holden's duty as catcher in the rye.

CHAPTER 21

Summary

When Holden arrives at his apartment house, he discovers to his delight that there is a new elevator boy. This means that he might be able to slip in, see Phoebe, leave the premises and not be recognized by anyone.

He enters his apartment quietly, sneaks down the hall to Phoebe's room, remembers that she sleeps in his brother D.B.'s room when he is in Hollywood, goes into D.B.'s room, turns on the light and sees his sister asleep: "I went around the room, very quiet and all, looking at stuff for a while. I felt swell for a change."

Holden looks through Phoebe's notebooks and is amused to find that she is using a new middle name. She does not like the middle name Josephine, so she changes it to whatever she likes. This time, her name in the textbook is Phoebe Weatherfield Caulfield.

Holden enjoys reading the little inscriptions in Phoebe's notebooks: "I can read that kind of stuff, some kid's notebook, Phoebe's or anybody's, all day and all night long. Kid's notebooks kill me."

Holden wakes her up and she is delighted to see him. Their parents have gone to a party in Connecticut and will not be home until very late, so Holden doesn't worry so much about being seen by them. Phoebe tells him that D.B. may not be home for Christmas since he has to stay in Hollywood and write a screenplay about a love story in Annapolis. Holden is disgusted by Hollywood and claims his brother knows nothing about Annapolis.

Phoebe guesses that Pencey kicked Holden out of school. She repeats over and over: "Daddy's gonna kill you." She covers her head with a pillow and will not come out from under it. Holden argues that nobody will kill him, that he can go out West and find a job. Phoebe refuses to listen, so he goes to the living room and puts some cigarettes in his pocket.

Commentary

Here we have the reunion of Holden and Phoebe and it turns out to be somewhat disappointing for Holden. When his sister guesses, almost psychically, that he has been thrown out of school, she buries herself under the pillow and terminates the conversation. Holden's source of contact with love and support is cut off momentarily, although he tries several times to reason with her.

This chapter is important mostly because it shows us the human side of Phoebe. She is a normal, albeit intelligent and precocious, young girl and is not at all perfect. In the park, she has been followed by a boy in her class who apparently likes her, and to show her disapproval, she puts ink on his windbreaker.

Her conversation is very much that of a sister excited about seeing her brother: she talks rapidly about the school play she is in and the film she has recently seen.

Something in Phoebe prevents her from listening to Holden in his attempts to explain his situation. It is as if she has been this route before with him and is disappointed by his apparent failure at Pencey. Phoebe, no doubt, sees her brother in much the same way as he sees her: an idealistic version of reality. When each realizes that their ideal brother/sister is more human than ideal, the conversation comes to a quick halt.

CHAPTER 22

Summary

When Holden returns to Phoebe's room, she has removed the pillow but will not speak to him. Then, when he tries to initiate a conversation, instead of answering his questions she says only: "Daddy'll *kill* you." Finally she asks him why he flunked out again. He replies: "It was one of the worst schools I ever went to. It was full of phonies. And mean guys." He sees that Phoebe is truly listening to him and knows what he is talking about.

He relates several of the episodes that happened at Pencey and she tells him to stop swearing so much. When he says that he didn't like anything that was happening at Pencey, she replies that he doesn't like anything anywhere. That depresses Holden. He tries to tell her things that he likes a lot, but cannot think of any: "About all I could think of were those two nuns that went around collecting dough in those beat-up old straw baskets."

Holden remembers that James Castle, a student at Elkton Hills, had said something about another student, and friends of the other student squealed on him. A group of boys cornered James in his room and demanded that he take back what he had said. James was a slim, fragile boy, but he refused to change his story. They began to torture him, but instead of giving in to their demands, James threw himself out the window and died on the stone steps below. He was wearing a turtleneck sweater which Holden had lent him. The only punishment the boys received was expulsion from the school; they did not go to jail.

Holden tells Phoebe that he likes Allie, their late brother, and that he likes talking with her. She downplays the importance of talking with her, but he disagrees: it is very meaningful for him. She asks him what he would like to be and he answers:

> I keep picturing all these little kids playing some game in this big field of rye and all. Thousands of little kids, and nobody's around — nobody big, I mean — except me. And I'm standing on the edge of some crazy cliff. What I have to do, I have to catch everybody if they start to go over the cliff — I mean if they're running and they don't look where they're going I have to come out from somewhere and *catch* them. That's all I'd do all day. I'd just be the catcher in the rye and all. I know it's crazy, but that's the only thing I'd really like to be. I know it's crazy.

Phoebe's only response to this is that their father is going to kill Holden, to which he replies: "I don't give a damn if he does." He gets up from the bed where they are talking and decides to telephone Mr. Antolini, his English teacher from Elkton Hills who now teaches at N.Y.U.

Commentary

There is a progression in this chapter within the character of Phoebe: she is disappointed with Holden, but gives him the chance to explain what he likes in life and what he would like to do with himself. But she always returns to the position of "Daddy'll kill you." She is young and impressionable, but more than anything else wants to believe in her hero, Holden. So at the chapter's end, when Holden leaves her room in order to call Mr. Antolini, she calls him back briefly to boast of her newly learned talent: belching.

It depresses Holden that Phoebe criticizes him and fails to understand his dilemma. He sees her as the only person with whom he can communicate, and when this channel is cut off, he feels an on-rush of despair.

When Phoebe asks him to list all of the things which he likes in life, he is unable to do so. The only people he can think of in a positive light are those who have been kind or unselfish with him — those who are innocent, pure, and prepared to stand up for their beliefs. It is in this context that he thinks of the nuns and of James Castle. Holden is horrified that the tormenters of James Castle did not go to jail. But he knows that justice is rarely done and that society is made up of people who prey on other human beings.

Most significantly, we now have the full explanation of the novel's title, as hinted at in Chapter 16. Holden wishes to serve humanity by safeguarding the innocence and purity of children, by protecting them from the evils of life (as symbolized by the cliff). His role is thoroughly selfless and unselfish: the beneficiary of his good deeds would be society at large, not Holden Caulfield. What ultimately drives Holden mad is the realization that he cannot singlehandedly eliminate the corruption and vulgarity of the world. When he understands that he must redefine his purpose in life and shift the focus of his intentions to those areas where he can actually accomplish good, he is able to pull himself out of the despair and set forth on a new path in life.

CHAPTER 23

Summary

Holden calls Mr. Antolini and tells him that he has been expelled from Pencey. The man says he can come over right away if he wishes. Then Holden returns to Phoebe's room, where they dance for a while.

After a few minutes, their parents return home. Holden jumps in the closet just before his mother enters Phoebe's room. Mrs. Caulfield smells a cigarette and Phoebe says she lit one, then threw it out the window. Her mother scolds her, asks why the light was on, criticizes Phoebe's use of certain words (e.g. 'lousy'), and pesters her with numerous questions. Phoebe tries to get rid of her.

After their mother leaves, Holden comes out of the closet and is quite nervous. He prepares to leave but Phoebe wants him to stay. If he leaves, he might miss her play. Holden asks for some money, but when he finds out that all she has is her Christmas money, he does not want to take it. She insists and gives him everything. At this, Holden sits on the bed and begins to cry. This frightens Phoebe, who puts her arm around him and shivers.

Holden leaves the apartment without being seen. He goes

down the back stairs and almost falls on "about ten million garbage pails."

Commentary

The true nature of Holden and Phoebe's relationship is shown here as they experience deep emotion for one another. When all is said and done, Phoebe loves her brother very much and wants only the best for him. Holden wishes the same for her. It is a moving scene when the two of them sit on the bed, arm-in-arm, as Holden cries. Their emotions have been stripped of all pretense and inhibition; what they feel is genuine and real.

It is clear that Holden does not have a particularly close relationship with his parents. They inspire fear and tension in him, but we should recall that this novel was written before the social revolution of the 1960s and 1970s, when traditional authoritarian values were thrown open to challenge and change. Parents were not as casual with their children or as interested in encouraging open, free dialogue about problems. The value system was more rigid and people were judged more quickly. Once certain standards had been transgressed, a prescribed punishment was often in order.

CHAPTER 24

Summary

Holden takes a cab to the Antolini's swanky apartment on Sutton Place. Though Mr. Antolini is a college professor, his wife is very wealthy. When Holden arrives, Antolini has a highball in his hand and his wife has some coffee ready.

Holden finds him witty, but sometimes he is too witty. He tells Mr. Antolini about his courses at Pencey, and the professor shows a true interest in him. Holden discusses his class in Oral Expression, where each student had to give an oral presentation. Whenever the student strayed from his subject, the others in the class were authorized to yell "digression!" If one digressed too much, one received bad marks in the course. This is what happened to Holden.

Mrs. Antolini serves the coffee, then goes to bed. Mr. Antolini is not able to help Holden: "Frankly, I don't know what the hell to say to you, Holden." He mentions that he had lunch with Holden's father a couple of weeks ago and that the man is very concerned about his son. Antolini warns that Holden is "riding for some kind of a terrible, terrible fall. But I don't honestly know what kind."

Antolini thinks that Holden is one of those people who are looking for something which their own environment cannot provide and who, consequently, eventually give up looking. He believes that Holden will die nobly for some "highly unworthy cause." He recommends that Holden discover quickly what he wishes to do with his life, and then apply himself to his studies.

After a while Holden prepares for bed; he is to sleep on the living room couch. Antolini goes into the kitchen and Holden, exhausted, falls asleep. Then, sometime later, he wakes up suddenly to the feeling of a man's hand on his head: "It was Mr. Antolini's hand. What he was doing was, he was sitting on the floor right next to the couch, in the dark and all, and he was sort of petting me or patting me on the goddam head." Holden is horrified and, in his nervousness, puts his clothes on and leaves, despite Antolini's protest that he remain. Holden argues that he must collect his belongings at the station, and Antolini replies: "You're a very, very strange boy."

Commentary

This chapter gives us insight into Salinger's ideas about style. Holden talks at some length about his Oral Expression class and his disgust for the nasty tactic of being downgraded for 'digressing' during a speech. Clearly Holden is a mouthpiece for Salinger when he says: "This digression business got on my nerves. . . The trouble with me is, I *like* it when somebody digresses. It's more interesting and all. . . Oh, sure! I like somebody to stick to the point and all. But I don't like them to stick *too* much to the point."

This is the stylistic technique Salinger uses in *Catcher in the Rye*: he chooses his digressions very carefully so that the novel flows beautifully, without jerking or seeming unnatural. It allows us to see inside Holden's mind and follow the pattern of his thoughts. Since no one thinks in totally logical, sequential or rational terms, it would be false to present Holden's impressions from any other viewpoint than that of digression.

As for the episode with Mr. Antolini, two points are obvious: on the one hand, the professor represents himself as a judge or authority figure to whom Holden should pay attention, yet it is this very figure who frightens Holden with homosexual-like advances. On the other hand, it is possible that Mr. Antolini was not trying to seduce Holden, but that he felt deep sympathy for the boy. He may have felt that the sleeping Holden looked peaceful and free of anxiety — and that his expression while sleeping was child-like.

The point is, Holden was alarmed by this intrusion into his sleep and, perhaps justifiably, felt he could not stay in the same apartment as this man. Holden had trust and respect for Antolini, and it is this kind of "perverty" experience which undermines his faith in the adult world.

CHAPTER 25

Summary

Holden takes the subway to Grand Central Station, where he spends the remainder of the night. He wakes up at nine o'clock as the stream of business people rush to work. He has a terrible headache and is depressed.

Holden wonders if he was too hasty with Mr. Antolini. Perhaps the man was not making a homosexual pass at him. He picks up a magazine and reads an article about hormones: "I looked exactly like the guy in the article with lousy hormones. So I started getting worried about my hormones." When he begins to think that he is diseased and will die within a couple of months, he drops the magazines and walks outside for some breakfast. He goes into a cheap restaurant and orders coffee and doughnuts. But he is too tense to eat, so he settles for the coffee alone.

He starts walking up Fifth Avenue. But every time he comes to the end of a block and steps off the curb, he has the feeling that he'll never get to the other side of the street: "Then I started doing something else. Every time I'd get to the end of a block I'd make believe I was talking to my brother Allie. I'd say to him 'Allie, don't let me disappear.'"

He decides to hitch-hike out West and get any kind of job available, pretending to be a deaf-mute so that no one will impose conversations upon him. But before doing this, he wants to say good-bye to Phoebe and return her Christmas money to her. He walks to her school and writes her a note, telling her to meet him at the Museum of Art. He sees some obscene graffiti on the wall and detests the person who wrote it: "I thought how Phoebe and all the other little kids would see it, and how they'd wonder what the hell it meant . . . and maybe even worry about it for a couple of days."

While waiting for Phoebe at the Museum, he helps two little boys find the Egyptian mummies. Then, alone in the tomb, Holden sees more graffiti on the wall and is depressed that "you can't ever find a place that's nice and peaceful, because there isn't any." He fantasizes about life in his cabin out West, where he would live in harmony with nature and away from the mainstream of civilization: "I'd have this rule that nobody could do anything phony when they visited me. If anybody tried to do anything phony, they couldn't stay."

Finally he sees Phoebe approaching him, dressed in his crazy hunting hat and carrying a suitcase. She announces that she is going with him out West. He feels like fainting and snaps at her that she cannot come with him: "I thought I was going to smack her for a second. I really did. She started to cry."

When he tries talking to her, she refuses to speak. So he says that he will not go out West, but she throws his hunting hat at him. Phoebe is not interested in Holden's comments and, in an uncharacteristically sharp moment, tells him to shut up. This upsets Holden very much. He feels she has as much as sworn at him.

He walks to the zoo and she follows him. Gradually she becomes less angry with him and allows him to buy her a ticket for the carrousel. When she gets off the ride, she tells him she is not angry with him anymore. Then she kisses him, reaches into his pocket, pulls out the red hunting hat, and puts it on Holden's head because it has started raining. As she rides the carrousel again, Holden gets drenched by the rain.

But he doesn't mind: Phoebe is on her favorite ride and he is suddenly overjoyed with happiness: "I was damn near bawling, I felt so damn happy . . . I don't know why. It was just that she looked so damn *nice*, the way she kept going around and around. God I wish you could've been there."

Commentary

This is the last major chapter of the novel, and we see the progression of Holden's sickness — caused by both physical and emotional neglect. He notices that his mouth has sores, he feels like vomiting, he faints at the Museum, and so on. At the same time, he is desperate for a solution to his anxiety and dreams of happiness in an anonymous life out West.

The encounter with Phoebe pulls Holden back to safety. He realizes the depth of her love and devotion to him. She is the only one available to help him and offers herself as a companion through his sickness. When Phoebe strikes back at him, it is because she is hurt and confused. She wants to be with her brother and is too young to manipulate him through force. It is through her love and innocence, her childlike beauty and unspoiled caring that Phoebe, unknowingly, rescues Holden from oblivion. The world may be ugly and soiled, but these special qualities of Phoebe shine through. They give Holden something to believe in.

The episode in which Phoebe rides on the carrousel is an important part of the novel. Holden sits on a nearby bench and watches his sister and the other little kids. The music starts up and the children ride around and around: "All the kids kept trying to grab for the gold ring, and so was old Phoebe and I was sort of afraid she'd fall. . . ."

Throughout the novel, various images and incidents have developed the theme of catching and falling (Allie's catcher's mitt; James Castle's fall out the window; Holden's desire to be a catcher in the rye, protecting all the little kids from the perilous cliff edge). The main conflict within Holden is closely related to his theme: Holden is torn between the desire on the one hand to grow up and to "adjust" and on the other hand to stay a child, living in a world of security and innocence. He has perceived adulthood as a fallen condition characterized by evil, falsity and betrayal and so has tried to evade it by dreaming of retreating to the woods, living in isolation — even dreaming of dying. But in Chapter 25, when Holden rejects his desire to prevent Phoebe from reaching for the gold ring, it signals his coming to terms with his inner conflict. Through the example of Phoebe, he begins to be restored to a belief in life — to accept that living entails both pain and joy, beauty and ugliness. Holden realizes that risks must be taken if one is to grow: "The thing with kids is, if they want to grab for the gold ring, you have to let them do it, and not say anything. If they fall off, they fall off, but it's bad if you say anything to them."

Finally, the rain that pours down, soaking Holden, is

suggestive of his rebirth and of hope for his future: ". . . it began to rain . . . . but I stuck around on the bench for quite a while. I got pretty soaking wet, especially my neck and my pants. . . . I didn't care though. I felt so damn happy all of a sudden. . . ."

CHAPTER 26

Summary

In this last, brief chapter, Holden is in the hospital. He says he prefers not to talk about what happened in his life after the experience in the park. He does say, however, that he went back to his parents' apartment, became sick and was transferred to the hospital. He has plans for returning to school in the Fall, once he is discharged from the hospital, but when people ask him if he will apply himself to his studies, he replies: "It's such a stupid question, in my opinion. I mean how do you know what you're going to do till you *do* it? The answer is, you don't. I *think* I am, but how do I know?"

He ends his story by saying that it makes him miss people when he talks about them — even Stradlater, Ackley, and Maurice. His final statement of the book is: "It's funny. Don't ever tell anybody anything. If you do, you start missing everybody."

Commentary

The novel ends on a note of slight optimism about Holden's future, but more importantly, of realism: he knows that as a human being he cannot predict the future, but he has adjusted himself to a peaceful frame of mind and is capable of assessing life as each new experience presents itself. There is no gloom and doom, nor is there any sense of pity for him. We see a boy who has been to the depths of despair and who has, nevertheless, survived.

The Catcher in the Rye is an emotional, stirring novel that holds our attention from beginning to end. Perhaps it is the humor that helps achieve this. Certainly, Holden Caulfield is an engaging literary character: he is honest, vital and one hundred per cent human. We can identify with the emotions he feels, and his campaign against phoniness is something that many people might share.

Plot

Methods of Analyzing Plot

Two Basic Kinds of Plot

The *action* of a novel (or play) is a straightforward chronological account of what happens from one moment in time to the next; the *plot* of a novel (or play) is the artistic manipulation of the events that occur so as to achieve the sharpest dramatic effect.

A plot may be tightly or loosely woven in the treatment of its events. The tightly woven plot may be compared to a closely spaced row of dominoes standing on end. When the lead domino is toppled over, all the rest inevitably follow one by one. The sequence here is comparable to the chain of events in a Grecian tragedy such as *Oedipus Rex*. Once the initial action is taken, all else must follow. Thus when Oedipus the King determines to find out the cause for the plague upon his city, he is led by the logic of events to the inevitable discovery that it is he — a man who has unknowingly murdered his own father and committed incest with his mother — who has offended the gods and who must be removed before the city can thrive again. Each particle of evidence as it is revealed leads to the discovery of another bit of knowledge, and the dramatic irony of the play (based on the contrast between the audience's and Oedipus' knowledge) aids the impact of a great Grecian tragedy.

The loosely woven plot depends for its power on no such inevitable cause-and-effect chain. Typical of the loosely structured novel are such works as *Don Quixote, Moll Flanders,* and *The Adventures of Huckleberry Finn*. These books are usually called *picaresque* novels. As such these works present a series of episodic events as they occur in the life of the main character (or picaro) of the novel. Generally, picaresque novels are told in the first person, are realistic in language and events, and are critical and satirical of social castes and national mores. *The Catcher in the Rye* is, of course, more closely aligned to the picaresque tradition than the Grecian one.

Some Basic Elements of Plot

The heart of any plot is *conflict* — the struggle between two relatively equal forces. (There is no meaningful physical conflict if a grown man beats up a young child.) It may be helpful for the student to realize that there are four basic kinds of conflict. The most obvious is that between man and man (as when Mercutio and Tybalt duel in *Romeo and Juliet*). Another is that of a man with warring factions within himself (as when Hamlet both wishes and does not wish to kill his uncle, and both desires and does not desire to punish his mother). A third is the conflict of man against the forces of nature (as in Stephen Crane's story "The Open Boat," where four men attempt to keep a small craft afloat despite the overpowering force of the sea). Finally, there is the conflict of man against his society (seen in Nathaniel Hawthorne's novel *The Scarlet Letter*, in which Hester Prynne does not regret her adultery with the Reverend Arthur Dimmesdale as immoral but instead claims that their sin, despite the codes of society and the laws of the church, "had a consecration of its own"). These classifications should be helpful, but in using them students should remember that the conflict in every novel is more specific than general. To see the novel's structure clearly the reader must ask *what* particular forces are pitted against each other and *why* they are struggling to overcome their antagonists. In addition the student should remember that every important incident in a good novel is in some way directed at the dramatization of the central conflict. Finding that conflict, therefore, helps to clarify the parts of the novel in relationship to the whole.

If the heart of plot is conflict, the soul of conflict is *suspense*. Quite simply suspense is the artistic manipulation of events by which the author teases the reader into constant interest in the outcome of the conflict. At the height of the conflict, the *climax*, when the opposing forces seem to weigh equally on the scales of fate, the author often slows down the action. By his slow-motion revelations, he teases the reader into an emotion which combines both fear and hope. The good student should be aware that during the *rising action* of the novel, the author is driving his narrative toward a climax of plot and meaning (and these divergent climaxes may come at different, or identical, points in the novel). For that reason, it is important for the student to be able to defend his judgment as to the dominant conflict, and its climax, in any novel.

Questions and Answers on Plot
Question 1.
The Catcher in the Rye dramatizes a number of relatively minor conflicts and one central conflict (and climax). Discuss two or three minor conflicts and the dominant conflict.

Answer
A simple physical conflict occurs early in the novel when Holden fears that his roommate Stradlater may have made love to his date Jane Gallagher. There is not a great deal of suspense to this action, for the forces are far from equally matched, but the fight does show Holden's chivalric mentality, and the result shows how slight is the prospect of victory when the struggle is between a practical man and an idealistic one.

A second conflict is that which occurs between Holden and Mr. Antolini. Holden is appalled by perversion of any kind, and the thought that his former teacher may be a homosexual horrifies him. In the slight conflict between Holden and Mr. Antolini, Holden is victorious (in the fact that he does escape), but after his flight Holden wonders if he had really been justified. He remembers how compassionate Mr. Antolini has always been, and he concludes that he has no right to make a judgment on him.

A third conflict, far more important than either of the above, is Holden's general opposition to the mores of society itself. The hypocrisy of much of society appalls him, as when he condemns a former headmaster who was especially courteous to well-dressed, well-to-do parents and especially curt, but ever smiling, to less sophisticated and powerful parents. The pervading materialism of Holden's time disgusts him, and he comments upon the trivial meaninglessness of the lives of well-to-do people. The commercialism and falsification of Christmas (and the spirit of religion) makes him sick when he sees it. And always, for Holden, the falsity peddled by the movies – in their images of people and their lies about life – surrounds him. As a creature of his time, he cannot totally escape this falsity.

The dominant conflict in *The Catcher*, however, is that within Holden himself, and it concerns his opposing desires, on the one hand to grow up and to ''adjust,'' and on the other hand to stay a child and to live in a world of security and innocence. For him the adult life is a world of sex (which both frightens and fascinates him) and of compromises with evil. Yet it is this world that he must enter, and he knows it. However, he tries to evade this knowledge. He wears a hunting cap backward to assert his immaturity. He dreams of escaping to pastoral worlds of innocence in Massachusetts or in the West. He dreams of living in isolation, with only occasional visitors and a set of rules that would require truth and naturalness as a way of life. Yet he knows, even as he dreams, that he is dreaming, and he becomes more and more frightened, illogical, and hysterical as the trap seems about to spring. At times he even thinks of death as the way to escape his horrid fate. The climax of this conflict comes when he realizes that life is to be lived, with all its pain and joy. With this knowledge, Holden is liberated, even re-born, and he is deliriously happy.

Question 2.

What does Holden's obsession with the ducks in Central Park have to do with the central conflict of *The Catcher?*

Answer

On a number of occasions Holden wonders where the Central Park ducks go in winter. Finally, toward the end of the novel, Holden sets out to find the ducks.

Obviously the dark quiet of the lagoon and the park make a stern contrast to the lights and struggle and ''life'' of the city. To let Holden's trip in search of the ducks go at that, however, is to ignore his central obsession: what happens to the ducks in winter. Holden never finds an answer to his query. Why? The reason is that there are mysteries beyond explanation. One of these mysteries concerns the ducks. Another concerns the meaning of death. The manner in which Salinger interweaves Holden's bewilderment about these mysteries implies, rather humorously, the close connection between them.

Holden's fascination with these questions ultimately becomes an obsession with the mysteries of life and death. One of the mysteries of life – the reason for evil – he solves in the course of the novel when he realizes that evil is a part of life and to live fully one must experience the wounds and pain of existence. For the mystery of death, however, Holden finds no explanation. Because religion is silly to him, he cannot rest in the consolation that Nature or God will take care of all things. The asking of the unanswerable questions is a reason for Holden's psychological maladjustment. Perhaps it is better to avoid, as conventional people do, such embarrassing problems, for to ask the hard question is not easy. But if man's aim is knowledge, then some people must continue to ask the difficult questions. Which is better? To question and draw near madness, or to accept all things and be comfortably sane. That is the choice that faces Holden at the end of the novel. Neither alternative is good, so Holden may well be right to wonder which road he will take in the future and to conclude that he cannot tell.

Question 3.

Compare the picaresque aspects of *The Catcher* and *Huck Finn*.

Answer

As is typical of picaresque novels, *Huck Finn* and *The Catcher* are told in the first person (I) by the picaro (or rascal) who is the hero. The picaro narrates a series of his adventures in realistic language and detail. This kind of language in *Huck Finn* is present from the beginning in Huck's dialect and illiteracies, as is suggested by the opening sentence of the novel: "You don't know about me without you have read a book by the name of *The Adventures of Tom Sawyer*, but that ain't no matter." In *The Catcher* this realistic language is carried even further (for Twain eliminated obscenity from his character's mouths), and Holden obsessively, instinctively uses such words as "goddam" and "hell" and "crap" and "ass." The naturalness, the unconsciousness, with which Holden uses such foul language implies its commonness among his friends, but even more it suggests a child's innocence, rather than a man's vulgarity, on the part of the user. In the same way, Mark Twain and J. D. Salinger present their settings and events in realistic detail. Huck describes a town in "Arkansaw" as follows:

> All the streets and lanes was just mud; they warn't nothing else *but* mud – mud as black as tar and nigh about a foot deep in some places, and two or three inches deep in *all* the places. The hogs loafed and grunted around everywheres.

Salinger describes a cab smelling as if someone had just vomited in it, and the lobby of a hotel that smelled of millions of dead cigars. The major difference between the realism of events in Twain and Salinger is that Salinger depicts perversion and sexuality (though not in erotic sensational ways) while Twain's unconscious censorship kept Huck Finn from the bewilderment caused by sexual ideas and doubts. A partial reason for this dissimilarity is the difference in time and setting of the two works.

As picaresque novels, too, *Huck Finn* and *The Catcher* are episodic in the presentation of their narratives. That is to say, neither novel has events springing by causative logic out of each other. To put it another way, there would be no great thematic or narrative difficulties if, in *Huck Finn*, the Grangerford-Shepherdson feud was placed after, rather than before, the incident in which Colonel Sherburn shoots the drunkard Boggs. In the same way, Holden's dates with Sally Hayes and Carl Luce might easily be transposed.

Most important of all the picaresque aspects of the two novels is that both works are satiric exposés of national mores. For Twain, who felt that only through laughter was there hope of eradicating social evils, the lack of common sense was the besetting sin of his society. That lack of practical realism was shown in the folly of slavery – which asserted that a man could be a piece of property when good common sense proved he was more than that – but Twain indicted other follies of his time as well. Sentimental literature he exposed through the characterization of Emmeline Grangerford, who painted pictures (mostly black) and wrote poetry in which "She didn't ever have to stop to think. . . . She could write about anything you choose to give her to write about just so it was sadful." The fraudulence of monarchy and aristocracy he delineated through the two con men, the Duke and the Dauphin. Superstition and false religion he exposed constantly – as for instance when he depicted a revivalistic camp meeting in which the church-folk become so emotionally aroused that they lose all vestige of reason and become easy dupes of anyone who wishes to steal their money.

In *The Catcher* there is the same exposure of the foibles and frailties of man. Salinger, in truth, seems to be intent upon exposing national illness, so that Pencey Prep and New York City become microcosms (small universes) of the whole of America. That realm, says Salinger, is beset by hypocrisy, by materialism, by irreligion, by self-centeredness, by falsity and phoniness everywhere. Holden's pilgrimage is a search for love and honesty in a world in which these things have largely disappeared. Instead of seeking salvation in churches, men worship false gods in movie houses; instead of existing in humility, men live in the pride of wealth and the satiation of the senses. When Holden goes to Radio City, he sees actors, for commercial purposes, parading a lot of religious objects upon the stage, and for Holden, this action is sacrilegious. To him, the whole of life, as men live it today, is commercial, trivial, and aimless. Holden wishes for a better life and higher values, but his problem is that he doesn't know where he can find these things in his society.

Characters

Methods of Analyzing Characters

1. Analysis of Character Development

Henry James, the famous American novelist and critic, once noted the falsity of attempting to differentiate between action and character when he commented that character determines action and action illuminates character. James was right, for action and characters are but different sides of the same coin, but it is helpful at times, for purposes of discussion, to separate the two. It is wise, therefore, to remember that character is revealed in four basic ways: by what a character says about himself; by what other characters say about a character; by what a character does; and by what the author says about the character. Of these methods of character revelation, the most reliable is the author's statement about the character's virtues and faults, but the lack of subtlety in this method of portrayal has made the author's intrusive report (as seen in the novels of Dickens and Thackeray) an uncommon technique in twentieth-century novels. The least reliable source of character revelation, since few people are trustworthy judges of themselves, is the character's report of his own virtues or faults. (Thus some critics have found Nick Carraway, the narrator of *The Great Gatsby*, an unreliable witness in his claim that he is one of the few honest people that he has ever known.) The most useful mode of determining, in contemporary literature, the traits of a fictional character is, as with real humans themselves, by noting what the characters do. From their actions one can see whether characters evolve and change or remain fundamentally the same. In novels in which the character gradually evolves, the author often builds to a moment of revelation (an epiphany is what James Joyce would call it) in which the character sees his own nature, dilemma, or environment in a dazzling and even liberating vision. In *The Catcher* there is such an epiphany during the scene in which Holden Caulfield watches his sister ride the carousel.

2. Motivation

Characters act the way they do for reasons. It is the responsibility of the intelligent reader to be constantly asking why each character acts as he does, for in probing the motivations of the individual characters, the reader will uncover much of the theme of any piece of writing. As a matter of fact, the difference between the passive reader – who sees little but the story and is interested, like a small child, only in what happens – and the intelligent reader is that one question: Why? That question must be directed everywhere: Why is this incident preceded by this other one? Why are these characters so strikingly similar to each other in appearance? Most of all, however, the question "Why?" must probe the *actions* of the major characters. In answering that question about the characters of modern novels, it is sometimes a help (and sometimes, one must admit, a hindrance) to know a little about human psychology as interpreted by Sigmund Freud or Carl Jung. (A Freudian critic, though not a very good one, might well interpret Holden Caulfield's actions, despair, and ultimate ecstasy as the result of: 1. The rebellion against the materialistic father; 2. The rejection by the mother and the intensified need for maternal love; 3. The search for love and the eventual success of that quest through the recognition of the little-mother, Phoebe.) This knowledge is helpful because many modern authors draw upon Freud – one author has called him the Bulfinch of modern literature – for their motivations and mythology.

3. "Type" Vs. "Individual" Characters

The twentieth-century American author F. Scott Fitzgerald once wrote (in a short story "The Rich Boy") that if you begin writing about an individual, you will find that you have developed a type; but if you start with a type you will end up with nothing. The remark implies that in all beings there are distinctively individual qualities, but in individual men also there are traits that place them in categories. The problem of the author is to capture the particular individuality of his characters; paradoxically, however, when he best captures that uniqueness he delineates something universal. That, of course, is what J. D. Salinger has done: he has captured the uniqueness of Holden Caulfield, but in doing so he has depicted a modern type, the mixed-up adolescent. Despite this tendency of the individual to turn into a universal type when he is probed deeply enough, it is still helpful to remember that there are type characters (villains with mustaches) and individual characters (unique beings with strange mental and emotional quirks) and the two have different functions in literature. The type character is usually relatively simple in outline (as Babbitt, in Sinclair Lewis' novel *Babbitt*, is the type of the unthinking businessman), while the individual character is more complex (as Captain Ahab, in Melville's novel *Moby Dick*, is filled with the depths and paradoxes of human emotion and aspiration). Type characters at times seem to be mere abstractions (and in such a work as Bunyan's *Pilgrim's Progress* they bear such suitable names as Christian, Pliable, Obstinate, and Mr. Worldly Wiseman), but they are often used effectively to illuminate the ideas in which the author is especially interested. Individual characters, in all their complexity, tell us about the remarkable variety of man and at times remind us of Hamlet's comment:

> What a piece of work is a man! How noble in reason! how infinite in faculty! in form, in moving, how express and admirable! in action how like an angel! in apprehension how like a god! the beauty of the world! the paragon of animals!

4. Analyzing Character Relationships

Human beings put on a variety of masks at different times to cover their one real face. (Eugene O'Neill once wrote a play, *The Great God Brown*, to dramatize this idea.) The masks they wear reveal their relationships with other characters, so that Holden Caulfield wears one mask for Ackley, another mask for Mr. Antolini, and reveals his one true face to his sister Phoebe. The task of the perceptive reader is to see those masks, to understand the reasons they are put on, and to pierce beneath them.

Questions and Answers on the Characters

Question 4.

Discuss some of the major fantasies of Holden Caulfield throughout *The Catcher*, and show how these fantasies illuminate his character and at the same time are relevant to the dominant conflict of the novel.

Answer

A fantasy might well be described as a daydream that in some way dramatizes a psychological need or an obsessive fear. Two important fantasies of Holden's reveal his needs. One of these occurs after he is humiliated by Maurice. At that moment Holden desires revenge upon Maurice and all the "spiritual tramps" like him. In his need, Holden draws upon the dream merchants of Hollywood who commercialize conventional melodramatic dreams to satisfy man's need in this world for love, revenge, adventure, and life itself. A similar fantasy that satisfies a need is Holden's daydream about going out West. That daydream, of course, follows Mr. Antolini's betrayal of Holden, and the fantasy reveals Holden's complete disgust with the people of the decadent city. The images of the purity of Nature and the nobility of humankind when removed from the corruption of the city make a romantic vision which innumerable authors have conjured up over the centuries. The industrialization of civilization has not, however, ceased, and where Huck Finn, disgusted with "sivilization" could "light out for the territory," Holden's dream is impossible to attain. Holden realizes the folly of his dream from its beginning, but he only accepts its impossibility when he is sure of the love of Phoebe and, therefore, does not need the comfort of the dream.

Question 5.

Discuss Holden's various relationships with the members of his family.

Answer

Holden's parents are relatively well-to-do New Yorkers who seem to have only a casual interest in their children. Subconsciously Holden is aware of this rejection – a common one, the novel implies, on this level of society – and never does he even think of seeking the love he needs from his parents. Holden seems not to want even to think of them. Only when he's asked what he wants from life does he consider the possibility of a profession like his father's. In thinking of such a profession, Holden realizes that some lawyers may defend and protect the poor and the innocent, but on the whole he sees lawyers as materialistic creatures filled with their own self-importance. The vision is a judgment on Holden's father and a rejection of all he stands for.

For his living brother D. B., Holden's attitude is largely one of contempt. This is because D. B. went to Hollywood. When he did so he committed a double betrayal: to Holden, who needed him, and to art, through prostituting his artistic talent. Thus Holden is appreciative of D. B.'s visit to the Los Angeles sanitarium, but he expects nothing from D. B. On the other hand, Holden's brother Allie died young, before the compromises with life had to be made, and Holden remembers him in all his kindness. It is to Allie, therefore, that Holden prays when he has fears that he is disappearing.

Holden's relationship to his sister Phoebe is, of course, the redeeming one in his life. A young child with the innocence of youth, Phoebe still has a maturity, a maternity, that is well beyond that of Holden. She worries about her brother, and yet she needs him, and his love, as much as he needs her. Holden has the desire to give her parental protection, but he realizes that the best parent allows the child to take chances, to grow up, and he, therefore, decides not to keep her from grasping for the brass ring. When he makes this decision he rejects the role of the catcher and in addition affirms his own acceptance of his evolving maturity.

Question 6.

Most critics insist that Holden grows and changes during the action of *The Catcher*. Some critics, however, contend that Holden's desire to be a "catcher" is consistent and unchanging throughout the novel. Can this attitude be defended?

Answer

If one ignores the significance of the carousel scene and the symbolism of the rain, one might make a good defense of Holden's unchanging desire to be a protector of the young. To do so, one might insist that Holden's decision not to go out West is based on his desire to preserve the innocence of his sister. Thus when he goes home, it is not because he has decided to accept the inevitable fate of his own adulthood, but to protect his sister and to give her the love which she too will desperately need as she goes through the wounds of adolescence. Therefore, when Holden asserts that he does not know what he will do in his own future – whether he will adjust to reality and society or not – he is essentially insisting that he will continue to be the protector of youth, and will continue to go through the same kind of agonies that the book has so thoroughly dramatized. He has learned nothing – but in his inalienable idealism, he clings to the hope of a better, less materialistic and hypocritical, universe.

Meaning

Methods of Analyzing Meaning

Serious fiction and drama attempt to communicate some aspect of the meaning, or lack of meaning, of life. Everything else – plot, character, tone, style, setting – in a serious story is focused on this effort, so that when a writer discusses plot or character most intelligently, he inevitably illuminates meaning as well. On occasions, the central meaning, or dominant theme, is simple and obvious; on others, it is complicated and elusive. Yet no reader should rest content after reading a serious work of literature without trying to state (perhaps in a single sentence, perhaps in a long paragraph) the dominant idea which the author dramatized.

1. Explaining the Theme

A serious work may have a number of minor themes as well as one dominant one, and an escapist work may have no discernible theme at all. (The purpose of horror stories, for instance, is to make one shudder, not to induce one to ponder life or human nature.) In formulating a statement of the dominant theme, the student should be certain that his concept is general enough to cover all of the story; at the same time, the statement of theme should be so particularized as to illuminate only one especial work. In attempting to define the theme, the student should be sure to make a thoughtful comment. (For instance, the statement "Macbeth is about ambition" is too broad and imprecise to be worthwhile.) In addition, the student should avoid falling back upon moral clichés in attempting to come to terms with the theme. The use of such clichés shows a lazy mind, but even more, the phrases are seldom appropriate to more than a part of a work.

2. Relating Plot to Meaning

Though all aspects of a serious novel or play should serve to illuminate the dominant theme, the central conflict and its climax are often especially important in clarifying that idea. For that reason the student should make a skeletal statement (a sentence or two should do) of the action, conflict, and climax of a novel. Then he should ask what the action is dramatically implying about life, human nature, and reality. From this probing, the student should be able to form a hypothesis about theme; he should then test his hypothesis to see if it fits all the parts of a work. If it does, he has found a defensible statement of theme; if, however, any part of the work (and most especially the characters) seems inconsistent with the hypothesis, the student should either modify or reject it.

Questions and Answers on Meaning

Question 7.

Briefly describe the dominant theme of *The Catcher*.

Answer

The Catcher in the Rye dramatizes the difficulties of the sensitive individual who recognizes, as he matures, the ugliness and falsity which make up a part of life and who must then learn to cope with that knowledge. Minor themes within this dominant one include the alienation of the sensitive individual from his society; the difficulty, even the impossibility, of communication without love; and the contrast between conformists who unquestioningly accept the codes of their society, and rebels who question incessantly the values of their world. To fulfill his dominant theme, J. D. Salinger tells of the pilgrimage of a young boy, Holden Caulfield, through the nightmarish world of New York. Seeking beauty and love, he sees little in the adult world but falsity and obscenity, and he receives a series of betrayals of love. In his agony, he dreams of protecting children from the knowledge with which he is being confronted, and he resents the loss of innocence which he is undergoing. The world of reality disgusts him and he is tempted by the peace of death. In his greatest need, however, he gains proof of the pure devotion of his little sister, and the awareness that that kind of love exists, even in a soiled world, brings him ecstatic joy and a belief in the worth of life. Even more, he sees life as a pattern of continuity, and he recognizes that the chances one takes in grasping for the brass ring are a part of life. In taking those risks, one may be hurt, but each individual has the right to grow up (not to be overly protected) and try to grasp the total reality, which includes ugliness, of life. Recognizing these things, Holden rejects his desire to prevent his sister from reaching for the brass ring, and when he does so, he accepts life both in its sunny aspects and in its rainy ones. That joy in all of life implies hope for Holden's future.

Question 8.

Does this novel have any significance for adults?

Answer

Yes. The universality of the theme cannot be overstated. If adult society cannot identify with the struggles of the young attempting to reach maturity, then adult society has no hope of maintaining a position of leadership. Without leadership, institutions would no longer give direction but merely propagandize. Social progress and communication is a two-way street which demands that the young understand the old and vice versa. Holden's apparent growth in awareness and responsible acceptance is the most dramatic event in the book, but it must be matched by a mutual movement of comprehension on the part of adult society if it is to mean anything.

Style

Methods of Analyzing Style

The unique personality of an author, the special tone of his voice, makes for the style with which he writes. "Style shows the man," and as a man is a complex of traits, so style is a multitude of qualities. When a man has a strong personality, his style, either in his actions or his writing, will be so overpowering that it will be recognizable anywhere. William Faulkner and Ernest Hemingway had unmistakable styles in what they wrote. In life, men show their varying styles by what they choose to do and how they set about doing it; in literature, authors create their styles by what they select to write about, and by the language in which they express themselves. Certain aspects of language – diction, imagery, point of view, and symbol – are especially important in any consideration of an author's style.

1. Diction

Each writer chooses particular words and a particular level of language to express his ideas, and that choice makes for a particular quality of diction. Some writers, such as Shakespeare, are fond of using language drawn from a military vocabulary, and that choice is an aspect of their diction; J. D. Salinger is fond of using words drawn from a teen-age vocabulary, and that is an element in his diction. Generally speaking, it is useful to remember that there are three levels of language usage: the vulgate, the informal, and the formal. The vulgate is the lowest level of language, and in its use of colloquialisms and illiteracies is more often encountered in speech (and in fictional dialogue) than in writing; the informal level is that naturally used by intelligent people in their writing, and most magazines are written on various levels of informal usage; the formal level of language is most appropriate to ceremonial affairs and highly erudite publications. One scholar has aptly compared the levels of language usage to varying styles of dress: overalls (vulgate), business suit (informal), and tuxedo (formal).

2. Imagery

Imagery is the use of figures of speech (among them irony, simile, hyperbole, and metaphor) in order to bring vividness and emotion to factual truths. After Lady Macbeth and her husband have conspired to murder the king, Lady Macbeth often walks at night washing and wringing her hands, and at one point she cries: "Here's the smell of blood still: all the perfumes of Arabia will not sweeten this little hand." The gross exaggeration illuminates Lady Macbeth's tormented mind better than any literal statement ever could. In the same way the use of simile (the comparison of two dissimilar things by the use of like or as), metaphor (the comparison of two dissimilar things by stating they are identical) and irony (the contrast, in simple form, between a thing said and a meaning intended) – these devices fuse meaning and emotion. Note how this fusion is suggested by the following simile from Joseph Conrad:

> His passion appeared to him to flame up and envelop her in blue
> fiery tongues from head to foot and over her head, while her soul
> appeared in the center like a big white rose;

by the following metaphor from Carlyle: "The public is an old woman"; and by the following ironic dialogue, following Huck Finn's statement he had recently been in a steamboat accident:

> "Good gracious! Anybody hurt?"
> "No'm. Killed a nigger."
> "Well, it's lucky; because sometimes people do get hurt."

These effective uses of figurative language should not make the student, however, think that figurative language in itself is an asset in writing. Stereotyped figures ("he worked like a dog") and self-conscious, strained figures are a mark of amateur writing.

74

3. Point of View

Technically, point of view in literature is the angle of vision from which a narrative is told. (Students often confuse the technical aspect of point of view with the general idea of an author's attitude toward life, his "point of view.") The most common points of view are the first person (in which the tale is told in his own voice by the narrator, and the author, typically, enters only the *narrator's* mind); the omniscient (in which the author knows all, enters the minds of *any* of his characters, and at times intrudes in the narrative himself); and the dramatic (in which the author tells his story as if it were a play and enters the minds of none of the actors).

4. Symbol

A symbol is an extremely complicated form of figurative language, and its purpose is to fuse thought and emotion. Essentially a symbol is a device by which one object stands for another (as the sound of the word "chair" stands for the object called chair, or the American flag stands for the American nation). In literary art, however, a symbol may stand for a number of related concepts (as the green light in *The Great Gatsby* stands for fertility and hope, for the concept of "go," and for the idea of the promise of the future). It is important to remember that a symbol is typically an oblique, indirect method of communicating an idea and an emotion simultaneously. The responsibility of the reader when he reads a work of art that makes use of symbols is to ponder the whole meaning of the work and to see how the symbols function in deepening the ideas and emotions of the work.

Questions and Answers on Style

Question 9.

What is the point of view of *The Catcher*, and why do you suspect Salinger chose this point of view?

Answer

The Catcher is written in the first person from the angle of vision of a sixteen-year-old boy. One reason that Salinger chose this point of view is undoubtedly his own fondness for children and his desire to capture the truth of a young boy's world. In capturing that reality he shows the rhythms of a young boy's speech; the vague way in which teen-agers trail off their ideas with "and all" or "something" or "anything"; the rambling quality of many of a teen-ager's ideas (so that *The Catcher* is full of the kinds of fascinating digressions that Holden defended to Mr. Antolini); the innocent obscenity of a teen-ager's talk; and the repetitions and insistences that show a teen-ager's insecurity and desire to tell the whole truth and nothing but the truth (as seen in Holden's continual phrases, "It really is" and "I really mean it").

By his choice of point of view (and the validity of the rhythms and language with which he reports that viewpoint) Salinger gains a closeness toward, and sympathy for, Holden that he could have gained by no other point of view. More important he is able to suggest with tremendous poignancy the dilemma of the young boy who is in between childhood and adulthood and is being torn apart by the problem of growing up. That torment grows increasingly during the novel, and stylistically Salinger reports this by the increased confusion and hysteria with which Holden wanders through New York. When he is with Sally Hayes, his words pour out, and he even begins, without being aware of it, to shout at her. Even worse, his frenzy causes him to use language and insults that he would normally avoid with girls. Even in the way in which Holden at times strives for formal language usage (as in his date with Sunny), one can see the contrast between the instinctive naturalness which Holden respects and the phoniness which his society says he should imitate. In some ways these two tensions – between formal and simple language – imply the essential conflict and even the theme of the novel.

Question 10.

Holden Caulfield makes a number of critical judgments upon writers and actors in *The Catcher*. Discuss some of them.

Answer

Among the writers that Holden admires are Ring Lardner and F. Scott Fitzgerald. One reason for his admiration of Lardner is undoubtedly the closeness of his own artistic technique – colloquial, full of the rhythms of his ordinary people, and filled with rambling digressions – to that of Lardner. Fitzgerald he probably admires – at least in his fondness for *The Great Gatsby* – because of the poetic sensitivity of Fitzgerald's art (and there are elements of this in Holden's writing) and because of the obsession with time which tormented Fitzgerald as much as it does Holden. In addition, the hero of *The Great Gatsby* dreamed of recapturing the past, and set out to actually do this in his attempt to recapture his fairy princess Daisy, and Holden, too, until he accepts continuity, wishes to hold back the clock. The difference between Holden's fate and that of Jay Gatz is that Gatz was killed soon after he entered the world of reality and discovered "What a grotesque thing a rose is" while Holden has accepted reality, and evolution, and survived.

One author that Holden dislikes is Ernest Hemingway. Probably this is because Holden feels that Hemingway is romantic and dishonest in his reverence for the simple "dumb oxen" of the world. Even worse, perhaps, is the way in which Hemingway depicts the sensitive man's bravery and stoicism as he passes through the world. Holden, as he admits, is fearful of physical violence, and he is more prone to pour out his troubles than to hold them stoically in. Holden's problem is that he can find few people to listen, for few people care.

Among the show-people whom Holden sees are the piano player Ernie and the actors Alfred Lunt and Lynn Fontanne. All of these have been at one time excellent in their fields, but over the course of time he feels that they have gained such adulation from their audiences that they have lost simplicity and honesty in their performances. Tragically enough, however, they are not even aware of what has happened to their art. Thus they continue on, becoming more and more pretentious and recognizing that fact less and less. Holden's comment shows his own respect for honesty, spontaneity, and naturalness in art, and it shows his awareness of the dangers that beset the modern artist. It is best to perform for one's self-respect and not to set one's course by the acclaim of audiences.

*J. D. Salinger: Some Crazy Cliff

It is clear that J. D. Salinger's *The Catcher in the Rye* belongs to an ancient and honorable narrative tradition, perhaps the most profound in western fiction. The tradition is the central pattern of the epic and has been enriched by every tongue; for not only is it in itself exciting but also it provides the artist a framework upon which he may hang almost any fabric of events and characters.

It is, of course, the tradition of the Quest. We use the medieval term because it signifies a seeking after what is tremendous, greater than the love of a woman. The love of woman may be part of the seeking, part even of the object sought, for we have been told that the Grail has gender and Penelope did wait in Ithaca. But if the love of woman is essential to the seeking or to the object sought, we must call the search a romance. These two terms (quest and romance) distinguish thematic patterns, and have nothing to do with tragic or comic effects. Furthermore, the same plots, characters, and idioms might be employed inside either pattern. But somewhere upon the arc of the Quest, the love of woman must be eschewed or absorbed: the hero must bind himself to the mast, or must seek his Ducalinda because she is Virtue, not because she is Female.

There are at least two sorts of quests, depending upon the object sought. Stephen Dedalus sought a reality uncontaminated by home, country, church; for like Eugene Gant and Natty Bumppo he knew that social institutions tend to force what is ingenious in a man into their own channels. He sought the opposite of security, for security was a cataract of the eye. Bloom, on the other hand, was already an outcast and sought acceptance by an Ithaca and a Penelope which despised him. And, tragically enough, he also sought an Icarian son who had fled the very maze which he, Bloom, desired to enter. So the two kinds of quests, the one seeking acceptance and stability, the other precisely the opposite, differ significantly, and can cross only briefly to the drunken wonder of both heroes. Bloom, the protagonist of *The Waste Land,* the Joads, Alyosha Karamazov, Aeneas, Ulysses, Gatsby – these heroes seek acceptance, stability, a life embosomed upon what is known and can be trusted. Dedalus, Huck Finn, Ishmael, Hans Castorp, Huxley's heroes, Dostoevski's Idiot – these protagonists place themselves outside the bounds of what is known and seek not stability but a Truth which is unwarped by stability.

*By Arthur Heiserman and James E. Miller, Jr. From *Western Humanities Review,* X (Spring, 1956).

American literature seems fascinated with the outcast, the person who defies traditions in order to arrive at some pristine knowledge, some personal integrity. Natty Bumppo maintains his integrity out-of-doors only, for upon the frontier a man must be a man or perish. For Huck Finn both sides of the Mississippi are lined with fraud and hatred; and because the great brown river acts as a kind of sewer, you're liable to find murderers and thieves afloat on it – even the father whom you fled might turn up dead in it, as though the river were a dream. But in the middle of the great natural river, when you're naked of civilization and in company with an outcast more untarnished and childlike than yourself – *there* is peace. And in northern Mississippi, in the ante-Snopes era, frontiersmen conquer the wilderness using only their courage and their fury; and they behave, even when civilization has almost extinguished them, with the kind of insane honor that drives Quentin Compson outside of society and into suicide. And the hunter, as he tracks the great mythic bear or the incredible whale, must leave behind whatever is unnatural or convenient. Similarly, when the bull charges, you are faced with the same compulsion for integrity as is required by the wilderness, the whale, the bear, the river; and very often, the world so botches things that you must "make a separate peace" in order to maintain your moral entity intact.

All the virtues of these American heroes are personal ones: they most often, as a matter of fact, are in conflict with home, family, church. The typical American hero must flee these institutions, become a tramp in the earth, cut himself off from Chicago, Winesburg, Hannibal, Cooperstown, New York, Asheville, Minneapolis. For only by flight can he find knowledge of what is real. And if he does not flee, he at least defies.

The protagonist of *The Catcher in the Rye*, Holden Caulfield, is one of these American heroes, but with a significant difference. He seems to be engaged in both sorts of quests at once; he needs to go home and he needs to leave it. Unlike the other American knight errants, Holden seeks Virtue second to Love. He wants to be good. When the little children are playing in the rye-field on the clifftop, Holden wants to be the one who catches them before they fall off the cliff. He is not driven toward honor or courage. He is not driven toward love of woman. Holden is driven toward love of his fellow-man, charity – virtues which were perhaps not quite virile enough for Natty Bumppo, Ishmael, Huck Finn, or Nick Adams. Holden is actually frightened by a frontier code of masculinity – a code which sometimes requires its adherents to behave in sentimental and bumptious fashions. But like these American heroes, Holden is a wanderer, for in order to be good he has to be more of a bad boy than the puritanical Huck could have imagined. Holden has had enough of both Hannibal, Missouri, *and* the Mississippi; and his tragedy is that when he starts back up the river, he has no place to go – save, of course, a California psychiatrist's couch.

So Salinger translates the old tradition into contemporary terms. The phoniness of society forces Holden Caulfield to leave it, but he is seeking nothing less than stability and love. He would like nothing better than a home, a life embosomed upon what is known and can be trusted; he is a very wise sheep forced into lone wolf's clothing; he is Stephen Dedalus and Leopold Bloom rolled into one crazy kid. And here is the point; for poor Holden, there is no Ithaca. Ithaca has not merely been defiled by a horde of suitors: it has sunk beneath waves of phoniness. He does, of course, have a Penelope who is still intact. She is his little sister Phoebe whom he must protect at all costs from the phantoms of lust, hypocrisy, conceit and fear – all of the attributes which Holden sees in society and which Huck Finn saw on the banks of the Mississippi and Dedalus saw in Dublin. So at the end, like the hero of *Antic Hay*, Holden delights in circles – a comforting, bounded figure which yet connotes hopelessness. He breaks down as he watches his beloved little Phoebe going round and round on a carousel; she is so *damned* happy. From that lunatic delight in a circle, he is shipped off to the psychiatrist. For Holden loves the world more than the world can bear.

Holden's Quest takes him outside society; yet the grail he seeks is the world and the grail is full of love. To be a catcher in the rye in this world is possible only at the price of leaving it. To be good is to be a "case," a "bad boy" who confounds the society of men. So Holden seeks the one role which would allow him to be a catcher, and that role is the role of the child. As a child, he would be condoned, for a child is a sort of savage and a pariah because he is innocent and good. But it is Holden's tragedy that he is sixteen, and like Wordsworth he can never be less. In childhood he had what he is now seeking – non-phoniness, truth, innocence. He can find it now only in Phoebe and in his dead brother Allie's baseball mitt, in a red hunting cap and the tender little nuns. Still, unlike all of us, Holden refuses to compromise with adulthood and its necessary adulteries; and his heroism drives him berserk. Huck Finn had the Mississippi and at the end of the Mississippi he had the wild west beyond Arkansas. The hero of *The Waste Land* had Shantih, the peace which passes human understanding. Bloom had Molly and his own ignorance; Dedalus had Paris and Zurich. But for Holden, there is no place to go. . . .

The flight out of the world, out of the ordinary, and into an Eden of innocence or childhood is a common flight indeed, and it is one which Salinger's heroes are constantly attempting. But Salinger's childism is consubstantial with his concern for love and neurosis. Adultism is precisely "the suffering of being unable to love," and it is that which produces neurosis. Everyone able to love in Salinger's stories is either a child or a man influenced by a child. All the adults not informed by love and innocence are by definition phonies and prostitutes. "You take adults, they always look lousy when they're asleep with their mouths open, but kids don't . . . They look all right." Kids like Phoebe shut up when they haven't anything to say. They even say "thank you" when you tighten their skates, and they don't go behind a post to button their pants. The nuns expect no swanky lunches after standing on a corner to collect money. Young James Castle would not go back on his word even though he had to jump from a window to keep it.

Holden is the kind of person who feels sorry for the teachers who have to flunk him. He fears for the ducks when the lagoon freezes over, for he is a duck himself with no place to go. He must enter his own home like a crook, lying to elevator boys and tiptoeing past bedrooms. His dad "will kill" him and his mother will weep for his incorrigible "laziness." He wants only to pretend he is a deaf-mute and live as a hermit filling-station operator in Colorado, but he winds up where the frontier ends, California, in an institution for sick rich kids. And we can see, on the final note of irony in the book, that that frontier west which represented escape from "sivilization" for Huck Finn has ended by becoming the symbol for depravity and phoniness in our national shrine at Hollywood. . . .

It is . . . poignance which characterizes all of Salinger's humor, this catch in the throat that accompanies all of the laughs. Holden Caulfield is no clown nor is he a tragic hero; he is a sixteen-year-old lad whose vivid encounter with everyday life is tragically humorous – or humorously tragic. At the end of the novel, as we leave Holden in the psychiatric ward of the California hospital, we come to the realization that the abundant and richly varied humor of the novel has reenforced the serious intensity of Holden's frantic flight from Adultism and his frenzied search for the genuine in a terrifying phony world.

Holden Caulfield, like Huckleberry Finn, tells his own story and it is in the language of the telling in both books that a great part of the humor lies. In the nineteenth century, Huck began, "You don't know about me without you have read a book by the name of *The Adventures of Tom Sawyer*: but that ain't no matter." The English of Huck's twentieth century counterpart, Holden Caulfield, is perhaps more correct but none-the-less distinctive: "If you really want to hear about it, the first thing you'll probably want to know is where I was born, and what my lousy childhood was like, and how my parents were occupied and all before they had me, and all that David Copperfield kind of crap, but I don't feel like going into it, if you want to know the truth."

The skepticism inherent in that casual phrase, "if you want to know the truth," suggesting that as a matter of fact in the world of Holden Caulfield very few people do, characterizes this sixteen-year-old "crazy mixed up kid" more sharply and vividly than pages of character "analysis" possibly could. In a similar manner Huck's "that ain't no matter" speaks volumes for his relationship to the alien adult world in which he finds himself a sojourner. But if these two boys lay their souls bare by their own voices, in doing so they provoke smiles at their mishandling and sometimes downright mangling of the English language.

Huck's spelling of *sivilization* gives the word a look which makes what it stands for understandably distasteful. Holden's incorrectness frequently appears to be a straining after correctness ("She'd give Allie or I a push. . . .") which suggests a subconscious will to non-conformity. But the similarities of language of Huck and Holden are balanced by marked differences. Both boys are fugitives from education, but Holden has suffered more of the evil than Huck. Holden's best subject in the several schools he has tolerated briefly is English. And, too, Holden is a child of the twentieth century. Mark Twain himself would probably be startled not at the frankness of Holden's language but at the daring of J. D. Salinger in copying it so faithfully.

But of course neither J. D. Salinger nor Mark Twain really "copied" anything. Their books would be unreadable had they merely recorded intact the language of a real-life Huck and a real-life Holden. Their genius lies in their mastery of the technique of first person narration which through meticulous selection, creates vividly the illusion of life: gradually and subtly their narrators emerge and stand revealed, stripped to their innermost beings. It is a mark of their creators' mastery that Huck and Holden appear to reveal themselves.

It is not the least surprising aspect of *The Catcher in the Rye* that trite expressions and metaphors with which we are all familiar and even bored turn out, when emerging from the mouth of a sixteen-year-old, to be funny. The unimaginative repetition of identical expressions in countless situations intensifies the humor. The things in Holden's world are always jumping up and down or bouncing or scattering "like madmen." Holden always lets us know when he has insight into the absurdity of the endless absurd situations which make up the life of a sixteen-year-old by exclaiming, "It killed me." In a phony world Holden feels compelled to reenforce his sincerity and truthfulness constantly with, "It really is" or "It really did." Incongruously the adjective "old" serves as a term of endearment, from "old" Thomas Hardy to "old" Phoebe. And many of the things Holden does, he does, ambiguously, "like a bastard."

Holden is a master of the ludicrous irrelevancy. Indeed, a large part of *The Catcher in the Rye* consists of the relevantly irrelevant. On the opening page, Holden says, "I'm not going to tell you my whole goddam autobiography or anything. I'll just tell you about this madman stuff that happened to me around last Christmas. . . ." By the time we have finished *Catcher* we feel that we know Holden as thoroughly as any biography could reveal him, and one of the reasons is that he has not hesitated to follow in his tale wherever whim and fancy lead him. For example, in the early part of the novel, Holden goes at some length into the history of the Ossenburger Memorial Wing of the new dorms, his place of residence. Ossenburger, we are told, was the Pencey alumnus who made a "pot of dough" in the undertaking business, and who, after giving money to Pencey, gave a speech in chapel "that lasted about ten hours." "He told us we should always pray to God – talk to Him and all – wherever we were. He told us we ought to think of Jesus as our buddy and all. He said *he* talked to Jesus all of the time. Even when he was driving his car. That killed me. I can just see the big phony bastard shifting into first gear and asking Jesus to send him a few more stiffs." Ossenburger, of course, has nothing to do, directly, with the "madman stuff" that happened to Holden around Christmas; but Holden's value judgment of the phony Ossenburger is certainly relevant to Salinger's purpose, the revelation of Holden's character.

When Holden refuses to express aggressive dislike of the repulsive Ackley, the pimply boy whose teeth "looked mossy and awful," he is not being facetious nor is he lying. He is simply expressing an innocence incapable of genuine hatred. Holden does not suffer from the inability to love, but he does despair of finding a place to bestow his love. The depth of Holden's capacity for love is revealed in his final words, as he sits in the psychiatric ward musing over his nightmarish adventures: "If you want to know the truth, I don't *know* what I think about it. I'm sorry I told so many people about it. About all I know is, I sort of miss everybody I told about. Even old Stradlater and Ackley, for instance. I think I even miss that goddam Maurice. It's funny. Don't ever tell anybody anything. If you do, you start missing everybody." We agree with Holden that it is funny, but it is funny in a pathetic kind of way. As we leave Holden alone in his room in the psychiatric ward, we are aware of the book's last ironic incongruity. It is not Holden who should be examined for a sickness of the mind, but the world in which he has sojourned and found himself an alien. To "cure" Holden, he must be given the contagious, almost universal disease of phony adultism; he must be pushed over that "crazy cliff."

*The Language of *The Catcher in the Rye*

A study of the language of J. D. Salinger's *The Catcher in the Rye* can be justified not only on the basis of literary interest, but also on the basis of linguistic significance. Today we study *The Adventures of Huckleberry Finn* (with which many critics have compared *The Catcher in the Rye*) not only as a great work of literary art, but as a valuable study in 1884 dialect. In coming decades, *The Catcher in the Rye* will be studied, I feel, not only as a literary work, but also as an example of teenage vernacular in the 1950's. As such, the book will be a significant historical linguistic record of a type of speech rarely made available in permanent form. Its linguistic importance will increase as the American speech it records becomes less current.

Most critics who looked at *The Catcher in the Rye* at the time of its publication thought that its language was a true and authentic rendering of teenage colloquial speech. Reviewers in the Chicago *Sunday Tribune*, the London *Times Literary Supplement*, *the New Republic*, the New York *Herald Tribune Book Review*, the New York *Times*, the *New Yorker*, and the *Saturday Review of Literature* all specifically mentioned the authenticity of the book's language. Various aspects of its language were also discussed in the reviews published in *America*, the *Atlantic*, the *Catholic World*, the *Christian Science Monitor*, the *Library Journal*, the Manchester *Guardian*, the *Nation*, the *New Statesman and Nation*, the New York *Times Book Review*, *Newsweek*, the *Spectator*, and *Time*. Of these many reviews, only the writers for the *Catholic World* and the *Christian Science Monitor* denied the authenticity of the book's language, but both of these are religious journals which refused to believe that the 'obscenity' was realistic. An examination of the reviews of *The Catcher in the Rye* proves that the language of Holden Caulfield, the book's sixteen-year-old narrator, struck the ear of the contemporary reader as an accurate rendering of the informal speech of an intelligent, educated, Northeastern American adolescent.[1]

In addition to commenting on its authenticity, critics have often remarked – uneasily – the 'daring,' 'obscene,' 'blasphemous' features of Holden's language. Another commonly noted feature of the book's language has been its comic effect. And yet there has never been an extensive investigation of the language itself. That is what this paper proposes to do.

Even though Holden's language is authentic teenage speech, recording it was certainly not the major intention of Salinger. He was faced with the artistic task of creating an individual character, not with the linguistic task of reproducing the exact speech of teenagers in general. Yet Holden had to speak a recognizable teenage language, and at the same time had to be identifiable as an individual. This difficult task Salinger achieved by giving Holden an extremely trite and typical teenage speech, overlaid with strong personal idiosyncrasies. There are two major speech habits which are Holden's own, which are endlessly repeated throughout the book, and which are, neverthe-

*By Donald P. Costello. From *American Speech*, XXXIV, (October, 1959). Reprinted by permission from the University of Alabama Press.

less, typical enough of teenage speech so that Holden can be both typical and individual in his use of them. It is certainly common for teenagers to end thoughts with a loosely dangling 'and all,' just as it is common for them to add an insistent 'I really did,' 'It really was.' But Holden uses these phrases to such an overpowering degree that they become a clear part of the flavor of the book; they become, more, a part of Holden himself, and actually help to characterize him.

Holden's 'and all' and its twins, 'or something,' 'or anything,' serve no real, consistent linguistic function. They simply give a sense of looseness of expression and looseness of thought. Often they signify that Holden knows there is more that could be said about the issue at hand, but he is not going to bother going into it:

. . . how my parents were occupied and all before they had me (5.)[2]
. . . they're *nice* and all (5.)
I'm not going to tell you my whole goddam autobiography or anything (5.)
. . . splendid and clear-thinking and all (6.)

But just as often the use of such expressions is purely arbitrary, with no discernible meaning:

. . . he's my *brother* and all (5.)
. . . was in the Revolutionary War and all (6.)
It was December and all (7.)
. . . no gloves or anything (7.)
. . . right in the pocket and all (7.)

Donald Barr, writing in the *Commonweal,* finds this habit indicative of Holden's tendency to generalize, to find the all in the one:

Salinger has an ear not only for idiosyncrasies of diction and syntax, but for mental processes. Holden Caulfield's phrase is 'and all' – 'She looked so damn *nice,* the way she kept going around and around in her blue coat and all' – as if each experience wore a halo. His fallacy is *ab uno disce omnes;* he abstracts and generalizes wildly.[3]

Heiserman and Miller, in the *Western Humanities Review,* comment specifically upon Holden's second most obvious idiosyncrasy: 'In a phony world Holden feels compelled to reenforce his sincerity and truthfulness constantly with, "It really is" or "It really did." '[4] S. N. Behrman, in the *New Yorker,* finds a double function of these 'perpetual insistences of Holden's.' Behrman thinks they 'reveal his age, even when he is thinking much older,' and, more important, 'he is so aware of the danger of slipping into phoniness himself that he has to repeat over and over "I really mean it," "It really does." '[5] Holden uses this idosyncrasy of insistence almost every time that he makes an affirmation.

Allied to Holden's habit of insistence is his 'if you want to know the truth.' Heiserman and Miller are able to find characterization in this habit too:

> The skepticism inherent in that casual phrase, 'if you want to know the truth,' suggesting that as a matter of fact in the world of Holden Caulfield very few people do, characterizes this sixteen-year-old 'crazy mixed up kid' more sharply and vividly than pages of character 'analysis' possibly could.[7]

Holden uses this phrase only after affirmations, just as he uses 'It really does,' but usually after the personal ones, where he is consciously being frank:

> I have no wind, if you want to know the truth. (8.)
> I don't even think that bastard had a handkerchief, if you want to know the truth. (34.)
> I'm a pacifist, if you want to know the truth. (44.)
> She had quite a lot of sex appeal, too, if you really want to know. (53.)
> I was damn near bawling, I felt so damn happy, if you want to know the truth. (191.)

These personal idiosyncrasies of Holden's speech are in keeping with general teenage language. Yet they are so much a part of Holden and of the flavor of the book that they are much of what makes Holden to be Holden. They are the most memorable feature of the book's language. Although always in character, the rest of Holden's speech is more typical than individual. The special quality of this language comes from its triteness, its lack of distinctive qualities.

Holden's informal, schoolboy vernacular is particularly typical in its 'vulgarity' and 'obscenity.' No one familiar with prep-school speech could seriously contend that Salinger overplayed his hand in this respect. On the contrary, Holden's restraints help to characterize him as a sensitive youth who avoids the most strongly forbidden terms, and who never uses vulgarity in a self-conscious or phony way to help him be 'one of the boys.' *Fuck,* for example, is never used as a part of Holden's speech. The word appears in the novel four times, but only when Holden disapprovingly discusses its wide appearance on walls. The Divine name is used habitually by Holden only in the comparatively weak *for God's sake, God, and goddam.* The stronger and usually more offensive *for Chrissake* or *Jesus* or *Jesus Christ* are used habitually by Ackley and Stradlater; but Holden uses them only when he feels the need for a strong expression. He almost never uses *for Chrissake* in an unemotional situation. *Goddam* is Holden's favorite adjective. This word is used with no relationship to its original meaning, or to Holden's attitude toward the word to which it is attached. It simply expresses an emotional feeling toward the object: either favorable, as in 'goddam hunting cap'; or unfavorable, as in 'ya goddam moron'; or indifferent, as in 'coming in the goddam windows.' *Damn* is used interchangeably with *goddam;* no differentiation in its meaning is detectable.

Other crude words are also often used in Holden's vocabulary. *Ass* keeps a fairly restricted meaning as a part of the human anatomy, but it is used in a variety of ways. It can refer simply to that specific part of the body ('I moved my ass a little'), or be a part of a trite expression ('freezing my ass off'; 'in a half-assed way'), or be an expletive ('Game, my ass.'). *Hell* is perhaps the most versatile word in Holden's entire vocabulary; it serves most of the meanings and constructions which Mencken lists in his *American Speech* article on 'American Profanity.'[7] So far is Holden's use of *hell* from its original meaning that he can use the sentence 'We had a helluva time' to mean that he and Phoebe had a decidedly pleasant time downtown shopping for shoes. The most common function of *hell* is as the second part of a simile, in which a thing can be either 'hot as hell' or, strangely, 'cold as hell'; 'sad as hell' or 'playful as hell'; 'old as hell' or 'pretty as hell.' Like all of these words, *hell* has no close relationship to its original meaning.

Both *bastard* and *sonuvabitch* have also drastically changed in meaning. They no longer, of course, in Holden's vocabulary, have any connection with the accidents of birth. Unless used in a trite simile, *bastard* is a strong word, reserved for things and people Holden particularly dislikes, especially 'phonies.' *Sonuvabitch* has an even stronger meaning to Holden; he uses it only in the deepest anger. When, for example, Holden is furious with Stradlater over his treatment of Jane Gallagher, Holden repeats again and again that he 'kept calling him a moron sonuvabitch' (43).

The use of crude language in *The Catcher in the Rye* increases, as we should expect, when Holden is reporting schoolboy dialogue. When he is directly addressing the reader, Holden's use of such language drops off almost entirely. There is also an increase in this language when any of the characters are excited or angry. Thus, when Holden is apprehensive over Stradlater's treatment of Jane, his *goddams* increase suddenly to seven on a single page (p. 39).

Holden's speech is also typical in his use of slang. I have catalogued over a hundred slang terms used by Holden, and every one of these is in widespread use. Although Holden's slang is rich and colorful, it, of course, being slang, often fails at precise communication. Thus, Holden's *crap* is used in seven different ways. It can mean foolishness, as 'all that David Copperfield kind of crap,' or messy matter, as 'I spilled some crap all over my gray flannel,' or merely miscellaneous matter, as 'I was putting on my galoshes and crap.' It can also carry its basic meaning, animal excreta, as 'there didn't look like there was anything in the park except dog crap,' and it can be used as an adjective meaning anything generally unfavorable, as 'The show was on the crappy side.' Holden uses the phrases *to be a lot of crap* and *to shoot the crap* and *to chuck the crap* all to mean 'to be untrue,' but he can also use *to shoot the crap* to mean simply 'to chat,' with no connotation of untruth, as in 'I certainly wouldn't have minded shooting the crap with old Phoebe for a while.'

Similarly Holden's slang use of *crazy* is both trite and imprecise. 'That drives me crazy' means that he violently dislikes something; yet 'to be crazy about' something means just the opposite. In the same way, to be 'killed' by something can mean that he was emotionally affected either favorably ('That story just about killed me.') or unfavorably ('Then she turned her back on me again. It nearly killed me.'). This use of *killed* is one of Holden's favorite slang expressions. Heiserman and Miller are, incidentally, certainly incorrect when they conclude: 'Holden always lets us know when he has insight into the absurdity of the endlessly absurd situations which make up the life of a sixteen-year-old by exclaiming, "It killed me." '[8] Holden often uses this expression with no connection to the absurd; he even uses it for his beloved Phoebe. The expression simply indicates a high degree of emotion – any kind. It is hazardous to conclude that any of Holden's slang has a precise and consistent meaning or function. These same critics fall into the same error when they conclude that Holden's use of the adjective *old* serves as 'a term of endearment.'[9] Holden appends this word to almost every character, real or fictional, mentioned in the novel, from the hated 'old Maurice' to 'old Peter Lorre,' to 'old Phoebe,' and even 'old Jesus.' The only pattern that can be discovered in Holden's use of this term is that he usually uses it only after he has previously mentioned the character; he then feels free to append the familiar *old*. All we can conclude from Holden's slang is that it is typical teenage slang: versatile yet narrow, expressive yet unimaginative, imprecise, often crude, and always trite.

Holden has many favorite slang expressions which he overuses. In one place, he admits:

'Boy!' I said. I also say 'Boy!' quite a lot. Partly because I have a lousy vocabulary and partly because I act quite young for my age sometimes. (12.)

But if Holden's slang shows the typically 'lousy vocabulary' of even the educated American teenager, this failing becomes even more obvious when we narrow our view to Holden's choice of adjectives and adverbs. The choice is indeed narrow, with a constant repetition of a few favorite words: *lousy, pretty, crumby, terrific, quite, old, stupid* – all used, as is the habit of teenage vernacular, with little regard to specific meaning. Thus, most of the nouns which are called 'stupid' could not in any logical framework be called 'ignorant,' and, as we have seen, *old* before a proper noun has nothing to do with age.

Another respect in which Holden was correct in accusing himself of having a 'lousy vocabulary' is discovered in the ease with which he falls into trite figures of speech. We have already seen that Holden's most common simile is the worn and meaningless 'as hell', but his often-repeated 'like a madman' and 'like a bastard' are just about as unrelated to a literal meaning and are easily as unimaginative. Even Holden's nonhabitual figures of speech are usually trite: 'sharp as a tack'; 'hot as a firecracker'; 'laughed like a hyena'; 'I know old Jane like a book'; 'drove off like a bat out of hell'; 'I began to feel like a horse's ass'; 'blind as a bat'; 'I know Central Park like the back of my hand.'

Repetitious and trite as Holden's vocabulary may be, it can, nevertheless, become highly effective. For example, when Holden piles one trite adjective upon another, a strong power of invective is often the result:

He was a goddam stupid moron. (42.)
Get your dirty stinking moron knees off my chest. (43.)
You're a dirty stupid sonuvabitch of a moron. (43.)

And his limited vocabulary can also be used for good comic effect. Holden's constant repetition of identical expressions in countless widely different situations is often hilariously funny.

But all of the humor in Holden's vocabulary does not come from its unimaginative quality. Quite the contrary, some of his figures of speech are entirely original; and these are inspired, dramatically effective, and terribly funny. As always, Salinger's Holden is basically typical, with a strong overlay of the individual:

He started handling my exam paper like it was a turd or something. (13.)
He put my goddam paper down then and looked at me like he'd just beaten the hell out of me in ping-pong or something. (14.)
That guy Morrow was about as sensitive as a goddam toilet seat. (52.)
Old Marty was like dragging the Statue of Liberty around the floor. (69.)

Another aspect in which Holden's language is typical is that it shows the general American characteristic of adaptability – apparently strengthened by his teenage lack of restraint. It is very easy for Holden to turn nouns into adjectives, with the simple addition of a -y: 'perverty,' 'Christmasy,' 'vomity-looking,' 'whory-looking,' 'hoodlumy-looking,' 'show-offy,' 'flitty-looking,' 'dumpy-looking,' 'pimpy,' 'snobby,' 'fisty.' Like all of English, Holden's language shows a versatile combining ability: 'They gave Sally this little blue butt-twitcher of a dress to wear' (117) and 'That magazine was some little cheerer upper' (176). Perhaps the most interesting aspect of the adaptability of Holden's language is his ability to use nouns as adverbs: 'She sings it very Dixieland and whorehouse, and it doesn't sound at all mushy' (105).

As we have seen, Holden shares, in general, the trite repetitive vocabulary which is the typical lot of his age group. But as there are exceptions in his figures of speech, so are there exceptions in his vocabulary itself, in his word stock. An intelligent, well-read ('I'm quite illiterate, but I read a lot'), and educated boy, Holden possesses, and can use when he wants to, many words which are many a cut above Basic English, including 'ostracized,' 'exhibitionist,' 'unscrupulous,' 'conversationalist,' 'psychic,' 'bourgeois.' Often Holden seems to choose his words consciously, in an effort to communicate to his adult reader clearly and properly, as in such terms as 'lose my virginity,' 'relieve himself,' 'an alcoholic'; for upon occasion, he also uses the more vulgar terms 'to give someone the time,' 'to take a leak,' 'booze hound.' Much of the humor arises, in fact, from Holden's habit of writing on more than one level at the same time. Thus, we have such phrases as 'They give guys the ax quite frequently at Pencey' and 'It has a very good academic rating, Pencey' (7). Both sentences show a colloquial idiom with an overlay of consciously selected words.

Such a conscious choice of words seems to indicate that Salinger, in his attempt to create a realistic character in Holden, wanted to make him aware of his speech, as, indeed, a real teenager would be when communicating to the outside world. Another piece of evidence that Holden is conscious of his speech and, more, realizes a difficulty in communication, is found in his habit of direct repetition: 'She likes me a lot. I mean she's quite fond of me.' (141), and 'She can be very snotty sometimes. She can be quite snotty.' (150). Sometimes the repetition is exact: 'He was a very nervous guy – I mean he was a very nervous guy.' (165), and 'I sort of missed them. I mean I sort of missed them.' (169). Sometimes Holden stops specifically to interpret slang terms, as when he wants to communicate the fact that Allie liked Phoebe: 'She killed Allie, too. I mean he liked her, too' (64).

There is still more direct evidence that Holden was conscious of his speech. Many of his comments to the reader are concerned with language. He was aware, for example, of the 'phony' quality of many words and phrases, such as 'grand,' 'prince,' 'traveling incognito,' 'little girls' room,' 'licorice stick,' and 'angels.' Holden is also conscious, of course, of the existence of 'taboo words.' He makes a point of mentioning that the girl from Seattle repeatedly asked him to 'watch your language, if you don't mind' (67), and that his mother told Phoebe not to say 'lousy' (160). When the prostitute says 'Like fun you are,' Holden comments:

It was a funny thing to say. It sounded like a real kid. You'd think a prostitute and all would say 'Like hell you are' or 'Cut the crap' instead of 'Like fun you are.' (87).

In grammar, too, as in vocabulary, Holden possesses a certain self-consciousness. (It is, of course, impossible to imagine a student getting through today's schools without a self-consciousness with regard to grammar rules.) Holden is, in fact, not only aware of the existence of 'grammatical errors,' but knows the social taboos that accompany them. He is disturbed by a schoolmate who is ashamed of his parents' grammar, and he reports that his former teacher, Mr. Antolini, warned him about picking up 'just enough education to hate people who say, "It's a secret between he and I"' (168).

Holden is a typical enough teenager to violate the grammar rules, even though he knows of their social importance. His most common rule violation is the misuse of *lie* and *lay*, but he also is careless about relative pronouns ('about a traffic cop that falls in love'), the double negative ('I hardly didn't even know I was doing it'), the perfect tenses ('I'd woke him up'), extra words ('like as if all you ever did at Pency was play polo all the time'), pronoun number ('it's pretty disgusting to watch somebody picking their nose'), and pronoun position ('I and this friend of mine, Mal Brossard'). More remarkable, however, than the instances of grammar rule violations is Holden's relative 'correctness.' Holden is always intelligible, and is even 'correct' in many usually difficult constructions. Grammatically speaking, Holden's language seems to point up the fact that English was the only subject in which he was not failing. It is interesting to note how much more 'correct' Holden's speech is than that of Huck Finn. But then Holden is educated, and since the time of Huck there had been sixty-seven years of authoritarian schoolmarms working on the likes of Holden. He has, in fact, been overtaught, so that he uses many 'hyper' forms:

> I used to play tennis with he and Mrs. Antolini quite frequently.(163.)
> She'd give Allie or I a push.(64.)
> I and Allie used to take her to the park with us.(64.)
> I think I probably woke he and his wife up.(157.)

Now that we have examined several aspects of Holden's vocabulary and grammar, it would be well to look at a few examples of how he puts these elements together into sentences. The structure of Holden's sentences indicates that Salinger thinks of the book more in terms of spoken speech than written speech. Holden's faulty structure is quite common and typical in vocal expression; I doubt if a student who is 'good in English' would ever create such sentence structure in writing. A student who showed the self-consciousness of Holden would not *write* so many fragments, such afterthoughts (e.g., 'It has a very good academic rating, Pencey' [7]), or such repetitions (e.g., 'Where I lived at Pencey, I lived in the Ossenburger Memorial Wing of the new dorms' [18]).

There are other indications that Holden's speech is vocal. In many places Salinger mildly imitates spoken speech. Sentences such as 'You could tell old Spencer'd got a big bang out of buying it' (10) and 'I'd've killed him' (42) are repeated throughout the book. Yet it is impossible to imagine Holden taking pen in hand and actually writing 'Spencer'd' or 'I'd've.' Sometimes, too, emphasized words, or even parts of words, are italicized, as in 'Now *shut up,* Holden. God damm it – I'm *warn*ing ya' (42). This is often done with good effect, imitating quite perfectly the rhythms of speech, as in the typical:

> I practically sat down on her *lap*, as a matter of fact. Then she *really* started to cry, and the next thing I knew, I was kissing her all over – *any*where – her eyes, her *nose*, her forehead, her eyebrows and all, her *ears* – her whole face except her mouth and all.(73.)

The language of *The Catcher in the Rye* is, as we have seen, an authentic artistic rendering of a type of informal, colloquial, teenage American spoken speech. It is strongly typical and trite, yet often somewhat individual; it is crude and slangy and imprecise, imitative yet occasionally imaginative, and affected toward standardization by the strong efforts of schools. But authentic and interesting as this language may be, it must be remembered that it exists, in *The Catcher in the Rye*, as only one part of an artistic achievement. The language was not written for itself, but as a part of a greater whole. Like the great Twain work with which it is often compared, a study of *The Catcher in the Rye* repays both the linguist and the literary critic; for as one critic has said, 'In them, 1884 and 1951 speak to us in the idiom and accent of two youthful travelers who have earned their passports to literary immortality.'[10]

[1]If additional evidence of the authenticity of the book's language is required, one need only look at the phenomenal regard with which *The Catcher in the Rye* is held by today's college students, who were about Holden's age at the time the book was written. In its March 9, 1957, issue the *Nation* published a symposium which attempted to discover the major influences upon the college students of today. Many teachers pointed out the impact of Salinger. Carlos Baker, of Princeton, stated: 'There is still, as there has been for years, a cult of Thomas Wolfe. They have all read J. D. Salinger, Wolfe's closest competitor.' Stanley Kunitz, of Queens College, wrote: 'The only novelist I have heard praised vociferously is J. D. Salinger.' Harvey Curtis Webster, of the University of Louisville, listed Salinger as one of the 'stimulators.' R. J. Kaufman, of the University of Rochester, called *The Catcher in the Rye* 'a book which has completely aroused nearly all of them.' See 'The Careful Young Men,' *Nation*, CLXXXIV (March 9, 1957), 199-214. I have never heard any Salinger partisans among college students doubt the authenticity of the language of their compatriot, Holden.

[2]Whenever *The Catcher in the Rye* is substantially quoted in this paper, a page number will be included in the text immediately after the quotation. The edition to which the page numbers refer is the Signet paperback reprint.

[3]Donald Barr, 'Saints, Pilgrims, and Artists,' *Commonweal*, LXVII (October 25, 1957), 90.

[4]Arthur Heiserman and James E. Miller, Jr., 'J. D. Salinger: Some Crazy Cliff,' *Western Humanities Review*, X (1956), 136.

[5]S. N. Behrman, 'The Vision of the Innocent,' *New Yorker*, XXVII (August 11, 1951), 72.

[6]Heiserman and Miller, *op. cit.*, p. 135. /174/

[7]See H. L. Mencken, 'American Profanity,' *American Speech*, XIX (1944), 242.

[8]Heiserman and Miller, *op. cit.*, p. 136.

[9]*Ibid.* /177/

[10]Charles Kaplan, 'Holden and Huck: the Odysseys of Youth, *College English*, XVIII (1956), 80.

NINE STORIES
Introduction

Between 1940 and 1953 J. D. Salinger published some two dozen stories. From this group he selected nine stories that he wished to save, and they were published as a collection in April, 1953. *Nine Stories* sold well from the first and held ninth place on *The New York Times* list of best sellers for more than three months. Since the publication of the paperbound edition in 1954, *Nine Stories* has remained in print constantly. All but two of the nine stories were first published in *The New Yorker*. "Down at the Dinghy" was published originally in *Harper's,* and "De Daumier-Smith's Blue Period" first appeared in the *World Review* in London.

Salinger's Major Creative Periods

Frederick L. Gwynn and Joseph L. Blotner have found it useful for critical purposes to divide Salinger's creative life into three periods. They have called the first period "The Long Debut: The Apprentice Period," and assert that it lasted from 1940 to 1948. Salinger's apprenticeship is notable mainly for its portents of the more important era, lasting from 1948 to 1953, which Gwynn and Blotner call "The Classic Period." It was during these years that Salinger's "major esthetic successes appeared." Among the "classic" stories are "A Perfect Day for Bananafish" (1948), "Uncle Wiggily in Connecticut" (1948), "Just Before the War with the Eskimos" (1948), "The Laughing Man" (1949), "Down at the Dinghy" (1949), "For Esmé – with Love and Squalor" (1950), and "Pretty Mouth and Green My Eyes" (1951). Two stories – "De Daumier-Smith's Blue Period" (1953) and "Teddy" (1953) – may be considered as examples of Salinger's third period, to which Gwynn and Blotner have given the elaborately appropriate heading "Seen through the Glass Family, Darkly: Religion Through Satire." Salinger's more recent work also seems to belong to this category.

The Theme of Childhood Innocence

The reader who is interested in pursuing the underlying themes that apparently link the nine stories may find it helpful to note that all but one of the stories in the collection (the exception is "Pretty Mouth and Green My Eyes") deal with children or adolescents. In general, these stories present the child struggling to relate his essential goodness (or innocence) to the phony adult world in which he finds himself. This is basically the same theme that dominates *The Catcher in the Rye*. Occasionally the innocent child is represented as a savior, or would-be savior, of the adult.

The Artist and Society

A second recurrent theme in these stories is the relationship of the artist to society. This theme is explored in "The Laughing Man" and "De Daumier-Smith's Blue Period." Without stretching the fabric of the story too greatly, one might also include "A Perfect Day for Bananafish" in this thematic group, for Salinger, like many other writers, sees the artist as a representation of the sensitive person driven by the need to communicate his perceptions to a not overwhelmingly interested public. The artist thus stands in the same relationship to society as the young and innocent child does to corrupted adults. Salinger provides no program for these sensitive souls in *Nine Stories*. There is some reason to suspect, however, that in the Glass-family saga, Salinger may offer some mystical, religious answers to the problems besetting sensitive people who find themselves living unhappily in an increasingly alien culture.

Mysticism and the Glass Family

The mystical, religious experiences that are captured in "De Daumier" and "Teddy" are echoed and reechoed in what we have of the history of the Glass family. The Glasses were first introduced to the public in "A Perfect Day for Bananafish," a story that describes Seymour Glass, the eldest brother, on the day that he committed suicide. Although the Glass family does not appear en masse in any of the nine stories, various members of this remarkable clan do put in individual appearances. "Down at the Dinghy" provides an insubstantial glimpse into the life of the eldest Glass sister, Boo Boo. The ghost of Walt Glass, who was one of Seymour's brothers, hovers over "Uncle Wiggily in Connecticut." These introductions to the still-growing legend of the Glass family may be read independently of the other Glass-family stories, but they gain in meaning and comprehensibility if they are read with the other available chapters in the cycle: *Raise High the Roof Beam, Carpenters and Seymour: An Introduction; Franny and Zooey;* and "Hapworth 16, 1924."

The reader who is puzzled by the ramifications of the Glass-family legend will find Arthur Mizener's sympathetic account in the Grunwald anthology helpful and Chapter 11 of Warren French's study most useful (see Bibliography). Mary McCarthy's attack on the Glass clan is recommended for a clearer view of what might be considered the excesses of late-Salinger. Mary McCarthy's views are perhaps substantiated by Salinger's story, "Hapworth 16, 1924." A rambling, excessively cute story, "Hapworth 16, 1924" seems to be a descent into a private world that the reader finds more bewildering than illuminating. The tight form of the earlier stories is replaced in "Hapworth 16, 1924" by a perilous formlessness. In reading late-Salinger there is a temptation to disregard the story as complete in itself and to view it rather as a source of further bits of information about the Glass family.

Salinger as Virtuoso

Considered independently of earlier and later publications, *Nine Stories* is the best available evidence that Salinger is capable of virtuosity as a writer, especially as a master of what is possibly the most difficult and demanding prose form, the short story. As Gwynn and Blotner have said, Salinger's immense popularity makes it necessary for anyone interested in contemporary literature to read his work with care, and there is no better place to start than with his "victories" – the short, satiric works that with *The Catcher in the Rye* have won him the reputation of being one of the best writers to emerge in the years since World War II. There is little doubt that

> . . . a half dozen of Salinger's short pieces of fiction are nearly perfectly organized works, with a variety of organizations, in which vivid human characters are involved in the basic human conflict between love and what Salinger's Esmé calls squalor – that is, evil, trouble, inhumanity, and sin – and in which the characters and conflict are embodied in original and memorable symbols that are often humorous, even as the dialogue and narration are always serious.

Summaries and Commentaries
"A PERFECT DAY FOR BANANAFISH"

Summary

"A Perfect Day for Bananafish," the first story about the Glass family to be published, appeared in *The New Yorker* in 1948. The story focuses on the thirty-one-year-old Seymour, eldest of the Glass children, and recounts three related events on one day of his Florida vacation with his wife, Muriel Fedder Glass.

In the first part of the story Muriel is seen waiting alone in her hotel room from about noon until nearly 2:30 P.M. for a call to go through to her mother in New York City. While she waits, she washes her hairbrush and comb, and reads an article entitled "Sex Is Fun – or Hell." When the call finally goes through, it becomes obvious that the Fedders are deeply concerned about their daughter's welfare. They question Seymour's mental health because of his allegedly peculiar behavior and because of a strange automobile accident he has had. Mr. Fedder's depressing talk with Dr. Sivetski about Seymour's symptoms has only heightened their anxiety. Mother and daughter also discuss some extremely mundane matters – the appearance of the hotel room, the clothes women are wearing in Florida, and the steps Muriel is taking to care for her sunburn. However, Mrs. Fedder's anxiety about Seymour is voiced recurrently, and she suggests to Muriel that Seymour should never have been released from the army hospital. She fears that he may lose control of himself at any time. Muriel, in an effort to reassure her mother, tells her that she has become friendly with a psychiatrist named Dr. Rieser, who is staying at the hotel. She goes on to ask if her mother knows where a certain book of German poems that Seymour had recommended is located. Muriel tells her mother that Seymour plays the piano a great deal and that for reasons of his own – Muriel conjectures he is ashamed of his paleness – won't take off his robe on the beach. She quiets her mother's last expression of concern by saying, "Mother, I'm not afraid of Seymour."

The scene shifts to the beach where Mrs. Carpenter is putting suntan oil on her daughter, Sybil. The child irritates her mother by intoning "See more glass." Mrs. Carpenter tells her very young child that she may run off and play while she herself goes off to have a drink with Mrs. Hubbel. Sybil delightedly runs off to Seymour's place on the beach. After a charming conversation, he agrees to go into the water with her to see if they can catch a bananafish. In answer to her questions as to what a bananafish is, Seymour explains their peculiar habits:

> . . . They swim into a hole where there's a lot of bananas. They're very ordinary-looking fish when they swim in. But once they get in, they behave like pigs. Why, I've known some bananafish to swim into a banana hole and eat as many as seventy-eight bananas. . . . Naturally, after that they're so fat they can't get out of the hole again. Can't fit through the door.

Sybil curiously inquires what becomes of them, and Seymour replies gravely that they get a dreadful ailment – banana fever – and die. Sybil and Seymour are buffeted by a wave, and the girl cries out joyously that she has seen a bananafish with six bananas in its mouth. Seymour kisses her foot and then announces that it's time to go back to shore. Sybil runs back to the hotel.

Seymour returns to the hotel a little later, and on the elevator greatly upsets a female passenger by asking her not to stare at his feet. When he gets back to Room 507, where his wife is asleep, he takes an Ortgies calibre 7.65 automatic out of his suitcase, checks the magazine, sits down on the bed, and then shoots himself through the right temple.

Commentary

The temptation in discussing this story now is to view it in terms of all that can be discovered about Seymour in other stories about the Glass family. This approach is justified by Buddy Glass's recent statement in "Hapworth 16, 1924"; he feels that he has been "installed, elaborately wired, and occasionally, plugged in, for the purpose of shedding some light on the short, reticulate life and times of [his] late eldest brother, Seymour Glass, who died, committed suicide, opted to discontinue living, back in 1948, when he was thirty-one."

However, the original readers of "A Perfect Day for Bananafish" knew nothing of Bessie and Les Glass, let alone of their remarkable brood, with the exception of Seymour. Thus, as an exercise in studying Salinger's techniques, it may be profitable to examine the story as if one knew nothing about the history of the Glass family – that is, as a short story that stands or falls on its own merits.

Using this approach, one may conclude with complete safety that the story is extremely well-made. The opening introduces enough mysteries to keep any reader's attention. Muriel's trivial activities and phone conversation are an ironic contrast to the events of the Sybil-Seymour sequence. It is only in the abrupt and shocking climax of the story that the threatening implications of Muriel's conversation with her mother are resolved.

There is more to the story than structural harmony. Salinger is a master of detail used to the best advantage. There is no room to waste in a short story, and Salinger – at least in the early stories – wasted none. Thus one is informed not of the hotel's name or of its exact location, but rather that it is in Florida. This is more than enough to evoke an image in the reader's mind. The reader is told why Muriel's call takes so long to go through – "There were ninety-seven New York advertising men in the hotel, and . . . they were monopolizing the long-distance lines. . . ." The stage is cleared for the reader to get a good long look at Muriel. She is portrayed as a well-dressed but in no way extraordinary young woman. These impressions are substantiated by countless details such as her choice of reading matter, which serves as an ironic counterpoint to the story as a whole. It is as out-of-tune with Seymour as is her complete misunderstanding of his reasons for not removing his bathrobe on the beach. Salinger emphasizes only those details that are relevant to his story. For a fuller description of Muriel, one must turn to *Raise High the Roof Beam, Carpenters and Seymour: An Introduction.*

Just enough of Sybil's relationship with her mother is portrayed to suggest a parallel between their disharmony and that of Seymour and Muriel. The few descriptive details devoted to Seymour emphasize his paleness, his gift for entertaining the young, and his extreme compulsiveness, which is best exemplified in his following an elaborate procedure in folding his bathrobe before going swimming. Although this compulsiveness may perhaps be disregarded as a hangover from routine army procedure, his peculiar reaction to the lady on the elevator cannot be explained so easily.

Perhaps Salinger's chief gift is his unerring ear for speech. One scarcely needs to hear more of Mrs. Fedder than her phrase about Seymour's "condition" – "It's sad, actually, is what it is" – to know just what manner of talkative, well-intentioned, but essentially stupid person she is. Described more fully by the matron-of-honor in "Raise High the Roof Beam, Carpenters," Salinger here deftly suggests her most salient characteristics through her conversation with Muriel. Mrs. Fedder's conversation with her daughter about Florida styles in the winter of 1948 is so perfectly female that it could have been tape-recorded. Salinger also catches accurately the accents of New York City in the ladies' talk. Sybil sounds like what she is, a girl of four or five, and Seymour is convincingly thirty-one and splendidly uncondescending in his conversation with the child. Again, it is only in the irritable tone he takes with his elevator companion that his presumed illness becomes totally apparent.

Salinger's eye for detail and his uncanny ear are perhaps responsible for his reputation as a virtuoso of the short story. Nevertheless, his stories have often been criticized for their lack of credibility. What does "A Perfect Day for Bananafish" add up to? Why does Seymour commit suicide? Can the reader believe that he was ill enough to take his own life? The evidence cited by the Fedders and backed up by Dr. Sivetski's dire prognostications are all that the reader has to go on, except for the incident on the elevator and the possibly macabre elements in the bananafish legend.

Are we to believe that Seymour is in an analogous position to the bananafish when they are stuffed with food? Is he stuffed with joy because his imagination stimulated the pure, unfettered imagination of Sybil to see what he saw, even though bananafish really do not exist? Is this the irretrievable moment of joy for him, beyond which there is no point in living? Or is he simply suffering from "battle fatigue" as the Sivetskis and Fedders of the tale believe? Or is there some implied parallel between what Sybil is and what she is to become – another Muriel? – that disheartens Seymour enough to make him take his own life? Does he find it impossible to endure the thought that Sybil's charmingly innocent approach to his ominous parable cannot last as she matures? Is Seymour's problem one of reconciling the illusions and imagination of youth with the harsh realities of adulthood? Or does he commit suicide simply because life with Muriel is impossible?

These possibilities and others must have suggested themselves to the first readers of the story. Curiously, even now, many years and many stories later, one is still not certain why Seymour took his own life. It is when one tries to clarify the meanings of Salinger's stories that one begins to look to the other chapters of the Glass-family legend for assistance. In "Hapworth 16, 1924" the unbelievably precocious seven-year-old Seymour writes his parents that all their children

> have a fairly terrible capacity for experiencing pain that does not
> always properly belong to them. Sometimes this very pain has been
> shirked by a total stranger. . . . Half the pain around, unfortunately
> belongs to somebody else who either shirked it or did not know how
> to grasp it firmly by the handle.

He goes on to say provocatively that he does not expect to live longer than "a well-preserved telephone pole, a generous matter of thirty (30) years or more. . . ."

This delayed revelation cannot be particularly helpful in itself, except as an indication of the peculiar, overwrought nature of this extremely brilliant child and man. Other stories in the Glass saga suggest that some kind of a joy-pain syndrome led Seymour to take his life. He is portrayed as being hypersensitive to happiness – specifically to the love that provokes some kinds of happiness. Seymour does not come to his wedding ("Raise High the Roof Beam, Carpenters") because, as the matron-of-honor acidly relates, he was "indis*posed* by *happ*iness." He later eloped with Muriel. In his diary in "Raise High the Roof Beam, Carpenters," Seymour states that he worshipped Muriel for the very house-playing qualities that make her seem like a less than lovely adult to the reader of "A Perfect Day for Bananafish." Seymour's central concern about Muriel, according to the diary, is that he doubts his ability to make her happy.

Neither "A Perfect Day for Bananafish" nor any of the stories so far published about Seymour and his siblings tells enough for the reader to reach final conclusions about Seymour's suicide. Perhaps we will never know, just as we can never be sure about the motivations of other people. In the meantime

Seymour's ghost is the central figure of the Glass-family saga – his poems, letters, and diaries form the reservoir upon which the other Glass offspring draw for spiritual sustenance. His personality in death, as well as in life, is so central to Salinger's apparent scheme that it becomes obvious why this story appeared first in time, and why it heads *Nine Stories*.

"UNCLE WIGGILY IN CONNECTICUT"

Summary

"Uncle Wiggily in Connecticut" is the second story in the collection that is at least partly related to the saga of the Glass family. The setting is suburban Connecticut on a bitterly cold winter day.

The story opens with Mary Jane's late arrival for lunch at the home of Eloise, her former college roommate. Mary Jane explains that she is on her way to Larchmont to deliver some papers to her employer, who is at home suffering from a hernia. The two women have more in common than a shared room in college – both failed to graduate, both are fond of alcohol, and both have married unsuccessfully, although Mary Jane's marriage soon ended in divorce while Eloise is still married to Lew. As Eloise and Mary Jane work their way through a succession of highballs, cigarettes, and mutually interesting gossip, it becomes clear that Eloise does not have any affection or regard for her husband, that she dislikes her mother-in-law, and gets along badly with her maid, Grace, and her daughter, Ramona.

Ramona comes in from playing, and as she is taking her galoshes off it becomes obvious that she is extremely nearsighted, secretive, and imaginative. She enters the living room and distinguishes herself, child-style, by energetically scratching herself as she greets Mary Jane. Eloise asks her daughter rather unpleasantly where Jimmy is, and Ramona, picking her nose, replies that Jimmy Jimmereeno is holding her hand. Ramona manages to explain – with some coaxing from her mother – that Jimmy is a black-haired, green-eyed orphan who carries a sword and wears boots. While Ramona is still standing there, the women rather desultorily consider the reasons for Ramona's inventing an imaginary playmate, concluding limply that it is probably because there are no other children in the neighborhood. Ramona then announces that she has to go outside again because Jimmy has forgotten to bring his sword in with him. As she leaves, Eloise convinces Mary Jane to call her employer and tell him that she is not coming. Eloise suggests that Mary Jane offer as an excuse that she has been killed.

By quarter to five in the afternoon, a far more drunk Eloise is reminiscing about Walt Glass, the only person who could ever make her really laugh because "he just *was* funny." She recalls the time that they were running to get a bus outside the PX when she fell and twisted her ankle. Walt promptly dubbed the ankle "Uncle Wiggily."

Mary Jane asks if Lew has a sense of humor, and Eloise indicates that if he does it is certainly not as good as Walt's was. As Eloise continues reminiscing about Walt, Mary Jane asks her why she has never really told Lew about him. Eloise replies that Lew is too unintelligent to receive such confidences. She explains that one reason she had married Lew was that he had said he liked Jane Austen. She discovered later that he preferred the works of L. Manning Vines, and had never even read Jane Austen. (For an extension of this literary debate see "Hapworth 16, 1924.") Mary Jane, however, persists in this line of inquiry, asking why Eloise won't at least tell Lew how Walt died. Eloise explains that Lew would "be a *ghoul*," but does finally tell Mary Jane that when Walt and another boy were wrapping a Japanese stove full of gasoline for their colonel to send home, it exploded, killing Walt and wounding the other boy. Eloise is weeping as she finishes telling the story.

Ramona is heard coming in, and Eloise asks Mary Jane to go and ask Grace to fix the child's dinner. Instead, Mary Jane returns with Ramona who announces that Jimmy has been run over and killed. Eloise decides to send Ramona upstairs to have dinner in bed on the pretext that the child is feverish.

At 7:05 P.M. Lew calls from the station, but Eloise invents a series of excuses to avoid having to pick him up. She rather sarcastically suggests alternative routes home, and when he apparently commends her wit, she replies, "I'm not funny. . . . Really, I'm not. It's just my face." Shortly after this conversation, Eloise refuses Grace's request that her husband be allowed to stay with her overnight because of the bad weather.

Eloise then goes upstairs and wakes Ramona, who is sleeping on the far side of the bed. Her glasses are neatly folded on the night table. Eloise roughly demands to know why Ramona is sleeping on the far side of the bed when Jimmy is dead and no longer needs the space. Ramona replies that she does not want to hurt Mickey Mickeranno, her new playmate. Eloise shrilly insists that her daughter get in the middle of the bed and sleep there. Standing by the door, Eloise suddenly rushes back into the room, banging her knee against the bed in her haste. She picks up Ramona's glasses from the night table and holds them against her cheek. Weeping, she repeats "poor Uncle Wiggily" over and over again. Finally she puts the glasses down, tucks Ramona's blankets in, and sees that Ramona is awake and has been crying. She kisses her daughter and then leaves the room.

Eloise staggers downstairs and awakens Mary Jane to ask her if she remembers a dress she had in their freshman year, which another girl had told her was the kind of dress no one wore in New York. Eloise, shaking Mary Jane's arm, asks plaintively, "I was a nice girl . . . wasn't I?"

Commentary

To understand Salinger's portrait of Eloise Wengler, it is necessary to consider the crucial role played by the ghost of Walt Glass, who was one of Les and Bessie Glass's seven remarkable offspring. There are scattered references to him in various Salinger stories not included in this collection. By combining them one may learn a little more about this man who may well assume the same legendary stature within his family as Seymour has at present. It will be recalled that Seymour is the eldest brother, followed by Buddy (the Salinger-like narrator of the Glass-family stories), Boo-Boo, their sister (see "Down at the Dinghy"), the twins Walker and Walt, Zooey, and Franny.

As a child of three, Walt was encouraged in a letter from Seymour to practice tap dancing.

> The age of three is no earthly damn excuse for not doing the simple things we discussed in the taxi on the way to the train. . . . If it is too "damn hot" to practice as reported, then at least wear your tap shoes fairly constantly . . . keep them on your haunting, magical feet for at least 2 hours per day! ("Hapworth 16, 1924")

In "Raise High the Roof Beam, Carpenters" Walt is described as Bessie Glass's "only truly light-hearted son." In "Seymour: An Introduction" the reader learns still more about Walt:

> Our younger brother Walt was a great bent-pin fisherman as a small boy, and for his ninth or tenth birthday he received a poem from Seymour – one of the major delights of his life, I believe – about a little rich boy who catches a lafayette in the Hudson River, experiences a fierce pain in his own lower lip on reeling him in, then dismisses the matter from his mind, only to discover when he is home and the still-alive fish has been given the run of the bathtub that he, the fish, is wearing a blue serge cap with the same school insignia over the peak as the boy's own; the boy finds his own name-tape sewn inside the tiny wet cap.

The same sense of interrelatedness that is suggested by Seymour's birthday poem helps to explain the events of "Uncle Wiggily in Connecticut" and the story's remarkable balance between sentimentality and irony.

Walt's death in what Buddy described "as an unspeakable absurd G. I. accident in late autumn of 1945, in Japan" is the spring-board of the story. Mary Jane's knowledge of Walt's importance to Eloise is one of the links between her and Eloise. Walt's personality, wit, and charm stand in contrast to the unflattering things Eloise says of her husband, Lew Wengler, whom the reader can only perceive as the most ordinarily affluent of commuters. Eloise's devotion (perhaps addiction is the more appropriate word) to the memory of her dead lover offers the key to her almost jealous refusal to let the maid's husband stay overnight, and to her ambivalence toward her daughter's imaginary playmates – the black-haired Jimmy, whose death is announced just after Eloise has told Mary Jane of Walt's death; and Mickey, whose appearance at the end of the story prompts Eloise's only genuine act of tenderness toward her daughter. (Ramona's myopia is intended, perhaps, as a symbolic equivalent to Eloise's own escape into alcoholic amnesia.)

Eloise seems to be an ordinary suburban alcoholic. Her language is vulgar, her manner bossy and unpleasant. The character of her friend and former roommate, Mary Jane, is never developed beyond the point of being a rather stupid foil for Eloise. Eloise's relationship with her family reveals her to be a careless housekeeper, neglectful mother, and hostile wife. As in all his best stories, Salinger manages to convey all this through conversation and through a limited number of actions. The speech of the two women is the kind of credible, italicized exchange of gossip and ideas one would expect. Progressing from one drink to another, they manage to arrive at what may be a "moment of truth." Eloise perceives in the unhappy Ramona a reflection of what she is and what she was. The story ends with the suggestion that Eloise's memory of the nicer person she once was, and her realization of the possibilities that still are open to her with her child, may help her to alter her life. But it is nothing more than a possibility, and one can only speculate about Eloise's future at a point in her life when she seems almost totally alienated from the world. The transplanted girl from Boise, Idaho is linked to the future only through her child, which some imaginative critics have speculated might have been Walt's.

Ramona herself never reaches the stature of a fully developed character. She is portrayed as abused and neglected. She does some things that Salinger apparently perceived as charmingly childlike – picking her nose, scratching herself, and making noise with her open galoshes. However, she, like Mary Jane, never seems quite real. The reader simply does not know enough about her. In spite of this, Ramona reflects the innocence, intuitiveness, and intelligence that make children the true heroes and heroines of Salinger's world.

"Uncle Wiggily in Connecticut" was the last story of his that Salinger permitted to have made into a movie. The result of Hollywood's transformation of the story into film was a tear-jerker. Salinger himself avoided falling into an abyss of sentimentality only through the clever use of irony, a device Hollywood has never learned to use well. In reading the story we may sympathize with Eloise, but we do not weep. She is too painfully human and inadequate to evoke more than our sympathy and our hope that she will awaken from her self-indulgence before she has completely converted the accidental destruction of her lover into the deliberate destruction of those around her.

"JUST BEFORE THE WAR WITH THE ESKIMOS"

Summary

After playing tennis five Saturdays in a row with Selena Graff, "the biggest drip at Miss Basehoar's," Ginnie Mannox decides that she is losing money by paying the cab fare home each week. All that Selena contributes are cans of fresh tennis balls. Ginnie raises the issue in the cab going home, but Selena protests that she has only thirty-five cents of the $1.95 Ginnie says is her share. After some wrangling, the gawky fifteen-year-old Ginnie accompanies Selena to her apartment.

While she goes off to find her mother and the money, Selena leaves Ginnie in the living room. A disheveled, myopic young man comes into the living room in his pajamas, thinking that his friend Eric has arrived. As he shuffles across the room, he tells Ginnie that he has "just cut [his] goddam finger." They discuss the possible causes of the cut while Ginnie decides he is "goofy" looking. Selena's brother tells Ginnie that he knows her sister, Joan, and considers her a snob. Ginnie retorts that she has never heard Joan mention him and informs him that her sister is engaged to be married. They resume the subject of his cut finger, and Ginnie advises him to put iodine on it. Something in her tone causes him to offer her the half of a chicken sandwich that he has in his room, but she refuses the offer politely. Selena's brother then asks her who Joan is marrying and confides to Ginnie that he had written her sister eight letters, none of which have been answered. When Ginnie asks him why he did not call up Joan, he tells her that he had been in Ohio working in an airplane factory. (He had quit college, and could not get into the army because he had a rheumatic heart condition.)

Selena's brother then walks over to the window and pityingly looks down on the "goddam fools," who, he explains to Ginnie, are "anybody." Speculating that all of the men on the street are on their way to the draft board, he tells Ginnie that their next war was going to be fought with the Eskimos and that only men over sixty would be used in combat. Ginnie gauchly remarks that at least he would not have to fight, whereupon Selena's brother decides rather abruptly to go and get dressed. As he leaves, Ginnie advises him to put a Band-Aid on his cut.

The young man promptly returns with the half sandwich, which Ginnie manages to taste before he leaves the room. She puts the sandwich in the pocket of her polo coat as Eric, a man of about thirty, enters the room. He looks as if "he might have just been in a play that closed in Philadelphia," or as if "he might have been with a law firm." Eric asks where Franklin is. When he learns Franklin is shaving, he starts to tell Ginnie that this has been the worst morning of his life. When Eric speaks, it is usually in verbal italics. It takes little coaxing from Ginnie to get him to explain that his apartment-mate, a writer "from Al*toona*, Pennsylvania – or *one* of those places," had walked out with everything he could lay his hands on. Eric goes on to tell Ginnie that he and Franklin are going to see Cocteau's "Beauty and the Beast," which he has seen eight times. He reveals that he met Franklin when they had been together in the aircraft factory. His own health, however, is, he explains, perfect.

When Selena re-enters with the money, Ginnie steers her into the hall, where she tells her she has decided she does not want the money after all. She asks Selena if she may call her and come over that evening. As she is leaving, she tells Selena that she has met Franklin and wonders how old he is and what he does for a living. Selena replies that her father wants him to go back to college, but Franklin feels that at twenty-four he is too old to do so. When the elevator arrives, Ginnie tells Selena that she will call her later.

On her way to the bus, Ginnie reaches into her pocket to get her change purse and finds the half sandwich. She starts to drop it into a trashcan, but instead, replaces it in her pocket. A few years earlier it had taken her several days to throw out an Easter chick that had died in the sawdust in her wastebasket.

Commentary

Salinger's short stories often seem to end without resolving the conflicts they present. One may read "Just Before the War with the Eskimos" several times without having any conviction at all as to what the ending is intended to mean. Similarly, one puzzles over what caused Seymour to commit suicide in "A Perfect Day for Bananafish." For that matter, what became of Eloise, in "Uncle Wiggily in Connecticut," after Mary Jane reassured her that she *had been* a nice girl? It is a tribute to Salinger's skill that he makes the reader care enough about his characters to go on puzzling long after the story has been laid aside.

Salinger sheds some light on his distaste for conventional endings in "Seymour: An Introduction" Speaking through Buddy, the narrator, he concludes that story by saying,

> I'm finished with this. Or, rather, it's finished with me. Fundamentally, my mind has always balked at any kind of ending. How many stories have I torn up since I was a boy simply because they had what that old Chekhov-baiting noise Somerset Maugham calls a Beginning, a Middle, and an End?

The conclusion of "Just Before the War with the Eskimos" leaves us with the problem of the half chicken sandwich that Ginnie puts back in her coat pocket. It is deliberately pointed out that several years earlier she had kept a dead chick for several days before throwing it out. What is the reader intended to make of the parallel between the sandwich and dead chick? Since the sandwich remnant is Franklin's gift to her, is it meant to suggest that he is similar in some way to the dead chick? If so, how is he dead? Is he symbolically dead because he was somehow destroyed by failing to complete college and by being rejected by the army? Has it something to do with his cut finger about which Ginnie is so solicitous? Or is it because of his association with Eric, who gives the reader the impression of being a homosexual – a situation that would preclude any very happy relationship between Ginnie and Franklin? Or are the readers of the story simply to conclude that Ginnie is a sweet and sensitive person?

Ginnie is far from being perfect. She is portrayed as a perfectly ordinary middle-class adolescent, with perhaps a few more advantages than most if attendance at Miss Basehoar's and weekly tennis matches followed by car rides are counted advantages. She is described as gawky, gauche, and large-footed. Her choice of a tennis partner seems guided by enlightened self-interest, since Selena's father makes tennis balls. Yet Ginnie can display gentleness and concern when confronted with frailty. The gentleness that is suggested by the saving of the dead chick is supported by her interest in Franklin's problems – his history, his cut finger, and so on.

Franklin, who is pitiful from the moment he appears on the scene in the living room, seems to serve as the analogical substitute for the chick. Disheveled and unshaven, he is redeemed from being totally repulsive by his frank and sometimes witty conversation with Ginnie. But the fact that he would choose to associate with Eric raises new problems about his character. Eric is irritatingly feminine – gushy, whiny, hyperbolic, opinionated – and probably overwhelming to people like Franklin. If Franklin is intended to be Ginnie's new dead chick, it may just be because he has, at twenty-four, come to associate with the Erics of the world instead of with the Joans, who never even answer his letters.

The slimness of the tale as a whole and its unresolved conclusion are compensated for by Salinger's grasp of the mores and language of New York's upper middle-class. Perhaps the story's greatest strength, however, lies in its excellent portrayals of children and adolescents. Of course Salinger is right in knowing that when Ginnie hears Franklin approach, she would cross "her long legs" and arrange "the hem of her polo coat over her knees." She is torn between family loyalty and sisterly delight when Franklin accuses Joan of being a snob. The conversation between Selena and Ginnie about the matter of who should pay the cab fare is brilliantly accurate. Salinger is a pleasure to read because he knows precisely how to record the world he knows best, even when this does not result in the most perfect Chekhovian organization and resolution.

"THE LAUGHING MAN"

Summary

"I," the narrator of the story, recalls the period in 1928 when he was a nine-year-old member of the Comanche Club, a group of New York schoolchildren who were led by a young man named John Gedsudski. Gedsudski seemed to the boys to incorporate in his person all the possible virtues.

Not the least of his talents was his gift for storytelling. Every afternoon as it grew dark Gedsudski would start a new installment of an enthralling story known as "The Laughing Man." The Laughing Man, as a child in China, was kidnapped by bandits, who placed his head in a vise. This treatment resulted in an appearance so horrible that the bandits kept his face covered with a mask of poppy petals. The mask exuded an opium odor that would reveal his presence.

As the Laughing Man grew older, he learned the ways of bandits, and eventually became extremely popular in the nation as a self-styled Robin Hood. On his frequent trips across the Chinese border to Paris, he countered and outsmarted his arch-enemies – Marcel Dufarge, "the internationally famous detective and witty consumptive," and Dufarge's daughter. Even though the Laughing Man grew wealthy, he continued to live simply with his four devoted accomplices: Black Wing, the timber wolf; Omba, the dwarf; Hong, the giant Mongolian; and a beautiful Eurasian girl.

One day, soon after the Comanches' baseball season had begun, the boys noticed that a girl's picture had been placed over the rearview mirror. Just as they had grown used to the picture, the girl, Mary Hudson, appeared in person.

For about a month Mary was present several times a week to participate in the Comanches' baseball games. Then one cold day in April the Chief parked the bus at the spot where they usually picked her up and continued with "The Laughing Man." In that installment the Dufarges captured Black Wing, the Laughing Man's timber wolf, and offered to set him free only if the Laughing Man would let them capture him instead. The Laughing Man loyally accepted these terms and agreed to meet the Dufarges at midnight in a forest outside of Paris to make the transaction. The Dufarges, however, leashed another timber wolf to a tree to fool the Laughing Man. But as soon as the Laughing Man had been tied to the tree he discovered the Dufarges' duplicity and pushed his mask off with his tongue. Mlle. Dufarge fainted. When her father saw her on the ground, he shielded his eyes and fired in the direction of the Laughing Man's breathing.

The installment ended there, and the Chief, after checking his watch, started up the bus. The narrator asked if he was going to wait for Mary, but the Chief did not answer. In the park the narrator saw Mary Hudson sitting on a nearby bench. When the game was called because of poor light, he saw her crying near third base. The narrator asked the Chief if he and Mary had had a fight, but was told simply to tuck in his shirt.

On the bus that night the Chief concluded the adventures of the Laughing Man in less than five minutes. Dufarge's bullets had seriously wounded the Laughing Man, and the Dufarges eagerly came to inspect the corpse. But the Laughing Man surprised them by regurgitating the bullets, an act that so shocked the Dufarges that they dropped dead. The narrator points out that the Comanches could have accepted that as an ending, but there was more to come. The Laughing Man lived on, lashed to the tree, while at his feet the Dufarges' corpses lay rotting. Cut off from the eagles' blood that normally sustained him, the Laughing Man grew weaker and weaker. Finally he appealed to the forest animals to get his dwarf, Omba. The dwarf arrived after a long journey, bearing the eagles' blood. But when the Laughing Man learned that Black Wing had been killed, his final gesture was to crush the vial of blood and remove his mask.

When the narrator was let off the bus he saw blowing around a piece of red tissue paper that looked like a poppy mask. By the time he reached home, his teeth were chattering so much that he was put to bed at once.

Commentary

Salinger's perception of the feelings and reactions of young people is perhaps nowhere handled more effectively than in this extremely well-constructed and well-written story. Salinger, like the narrator, was born in 1919, and attended a public school on New York's upper West Side. Whether the events of the story actually happened to him or not, he seems completely in control of his material. The story has the ring of authenticity, the appeal of the past revisited. The form of narration and the sorrowful mood are typical both of Salinger's work and of *The New Yorker*, where his best stories have appeared.

The conjunction of the ludicrous yet engrossing tale of "The Laughing Man" with the story of the love affair between John Gedsudski and Mary Hudson is an effective way of projecting emotions at the child's level of perception. The reader, like the Comanches, never knows exactly what is going on between John and Mary; he intuits it as the narrator does. The couple's break-up, mirrored in the abrupt and horrible end of "The Laughing Man," is poignant and touching.

To the narrator and the rest of the Comanches "The Laughing Man" is far more than a fantasy story. The boys become intensely involved in the reality of the narrative, for the Laughing Man's relationships to his friends and enemies seem to mirror the Comanches' own relationships to one another and to the outside world. The narrator considers himself a direct descendant of the Laughing Man. His real parents are, in fact, only bogus parents, and he is their imposter son. He goes along with their orders on the principle that he had best watch his step until the time when he can safely assert his true identity. Although the Comanches go through the motions of dutifully brushing their teeth and combing their hair, their real life is rooted in the courage, loyalty, integrity, and compassion represented by the Laughing Man. In this story, as in so much of his work, Salinger skillfully evokes the world of childhood as something quite distinct from the adult world. The narrator's vague perception of a change in the Chief's relationship with Mary, a change that is somehow connected with the death of the Laughing Man, leaves him with his teeth chattering. Salinger's understanding of the child's psyche prevents him from attributing more profound reactions to the narrator at this moment of crisis. He successfully conveys the child's sense of loss through the teeth chattering and through the piece of red tissue paper that reminds the narrator of "someone's poppy-petal mask."

Salinger's interest in portraying precocious children is mercifully suppressed in this story. The delineation of the young narrator's character is completely believable. Every action is meaningful, and every word spoken is appropriate. The narrator, for instance, could not be expected to see Mary Hudson as a three-dimensional person. What impresses him most is her extraordinary ability to play baseball. Even the rift between the Chief and Mary is seen in terms of baseball. When on the fateful afternoon Mary refuses to play and asks to be left alone, the narrator knows intuitively that she would no longer be part of the Comanche lineup. The real nature of the crisis is not for him to comprehend.

Its many virtues make "The Laughing Man" a story to return to and marvel at after concluding such a windy and coy ramble as "Hapworth 16, 1924." In fact, a comparison of the two stories would provide a better insight into Salinger's development than a host of critical commentaries.

"DOWN AT THE DINGHY"

Summary

This is the third story in the collection that deals with members of the Glass family. The central figures in "Down at the Dinghy" are Beatrice (Boo

Boo) Glass Tannenbaum and her son, Lionel, who is the nephew of the other Glass-family offspring.

At the time of the story, a day in Indian summer, four-year-old Lionel is the subject of conversation between the Tannenbaums' fat maid, Sandra, and the laundress, Mrs. Snell. Sandra is concerned and irritable for fear Lionel will tell his mother something, complaining that he seems always to be there, underfoot, silent, and listening. Mrs. Snell points out that he is a good-looking child, but Sandra predicts he will have a nose like his father's. She complains about being stuck in the country in October when she vastly prefers the city. Sandra asks Mrs. Snell what she would do if she were in her shoes, but does not get the answer because Boo Boo then comes into the kitchen to find a pickle. She hopes to use it to lure Lionel out of the dinghy in which he is now seated, having run away from home. Sandra says Lionel has already eaten the last pickle. Mrs. Snell then listens with great interest as Sandra and Boo Boo recall the other times in the last two years on which Lionel has run away.

Boo Boo leaves to go down to the pier. Lionel is sitting with considerable dignity in the dinghy and is not allured when his mother announces herself as Vice-Admiral Tannenbaum. Lionel insists she is a lady and nothing more. She manages to sound a reasonable facsimile of a bugle call with her mouth and tells Lionel she would be drummed out of the corps if anyone knew she had revealed the secret call. Lionel insists on hearing the call again, but refuses, in exchange, to tell his mother why he has run away.

Boo Boo tries a new tack, reminding Lionel that he had promised never to run away again. She adds that she is very lonesome without him, but he refuses to let her board the boat. By way of emphasis, he kicks a pair of goggles overboard. Boo Boo tells him they were Uncle Seymour's goggles and that by rights she should now drop the package she has for him - a key chain with ten keys - in the water. He asks her to throw it to him. She does, and he throws the package in the water. Then he begins to weep, and his mother finally gets into the boat and comforts him.

As she reminds him that sailors don't cry, except at disastrous moments, Lionel confesses that Sandra told Mrs. Snell that his father was "a big - sloppy - kite." Boo Boo flinches a bit, but upon inquiry discovers that Lionel thinks a kike is something you fly in the sky on a string. Boo Boo suggests that they drive to town to buy some bread and pickles. They can eat the pickles in the car, pick up Mr. Tannenbaum at the station, and then go sailing. Lionel agrees and they race up the hill. Lionel wins the race.

Commentary

In the much-too-long letter Seymour wrote his family in the summer of 1924 ("Hapworth 16, 1924"), he included some advice for his sister Boo Boo:

> my dear, darling, unforgettable Miss Beatrice Glass, please work harder on your manners and etiquette in private as well as in public. I am far less concerned about how you behave in public than

how you behave when you are absolutely alone in a solitary room; when you accidentally look deep into a lonely mirror, let a girl with stunning tact, as well as flashing, black eyes, reflect!

The recipient of this and other advice of a more practical nature was then four years old. Boo Boo did her stint on the quiz program "It's a Wise Child," on which all the Glass children appeared at one time or another, and served as a Wave during World War II. During the war she met a man named Tannenbaum whom she later married. The Tannenbaums have a home in Tuckahoe and a summer residence in New England. Lionel is the eldest of the Tannenbaums' three children. All these details can be garnered by the energetic investigator into Glass-family history. The well-informed reader may come to suspect the unseen hand of Buddy in the description of Boo Boo at the opening of "Down at the Dinghy":

> She was a small, almost hipless girl of twenty-five, with styleless, colourless, brittle hair pushed back behind her ears, which were very large. . . . Her joke of a name aside, her general unprettiness aside, she was – in terms of permanently memorable, immoderately perceptive, small-area faces – a stunning and final girl.

Aside from the confusion in the author's mathematics, which would make the time of the story 1945 and place Boo Boo's marriage in 1941 when she was a Wave, this is possibly one of the most irritating statements ever penned by Salinger about any member of the Glass family. The description makes Boo Boo seem thoroughly unattractive, while insisting that she is a "stunning and final girl." It is, in fact, a passage that might well have been eliminated in an early draft; the story itself tells us that Boo Boo is a most attractive human being. She is intelligent, patient, and affectionate with her child, who, even at four, sounds as if he is on his way to becoming as special and as difficult as his uncles.

It is a pity, perhaps, that one's knowledge of the history of the Glass family intrudes upon this story. For the purposes of the tale it is not very important whose goggles Lionel kicks overboard; knowing that they were Seymour's adds so much weight to them symbolically that one must pause and reflect on the meaning of this apparently not too significant detail. By inflating the importance of Boo Boo's appearance and of such details as Seymour's goggles, Salinger detracts from what would otherwise be a touching and trenchant glimpse of the world of the nearly assimilated American Jew, for whom anti-Semitism is only an occasionally ominous reminder of other times and other countries. In "Down at the Dinghy" Salinger has succeeded more in giving us a glimpse of the way of life of the assimilated than in adding to our understanding of the much larger social problems of which anti-Semitism is one part. In the context of this story Lionel's reaction to hearing his father described as a kike does not have any more importance than being told by a contemporary that he "stinks." It is one more bruise on his innocence, for which the remedy is pickles and Boo Boo's love. If the solution for the social issue were as simple as this story suggests, the world would be an easier place in which to grow up. Harmless semantic games (kike-kite) would eliminate every human friction. To put it another way, one can only wonder whether Boo Boo's "stunning tact" is quite the answer to her son's problem.

"FOR ESMÉ — WITH LOVE AND SQUALOR"

Summary

The time is early spring in 1950. The narrator has just received an invitation by air mail to attend a wedding in England on April 18. Although the wedding is one he would give almost anything to attend, a discussion with his wife makes it clear that he cannot. Instead, to celebrate the occasion, he makes a few notes on the bride as he knew her six years earlier.

In April, 1944, the author had been one of sixty enlisted men taking a specialized three-week, pre-Invasion training course, directed by British Intelligence, in Devon, England. On the last day of the course, the narrator entered a local church, in which the children's choir was about to begin practising. Pleased with the way the children sang, he was particularly taken with a blond thirteen-year-old girl whose voice stood out.

Seated in a civilian tearoom after the rehearsal, the narrator noticed the choir member, her five-year-old brother, and their governess come in and sit down. The soldier and the girl exchanged experimental smiles across the room. Self-confidently, the girl came over to the narrator's table and told him that she had seen him at choir practice. He noted that she chewed her nails and that she was wearing a military-looking wristwatch. When he complimented her on her voice, she told him that she planned to be a professional jazz singer; at thirty she would retire to her ranch in Ohio.

The girl informed the narrator that she had come to his table because he looked lonely; she was trying to learn to be more sympathetic. Esmé and the solider then exchanged names.

Their deeply engrossing conversation was suddenly interrupted when Esmé's brother, Charles, announced that Miss Megley wished Esmé to come back and finish her tea. Charles's wriggling led Esmé to tell the soldier that their father had been killed in North Africa. (She spelled out the "s-l-a-i-n," as she did all other words that she did not want her brother to understand.) Esmé informed the soldier that her father had been a very handsome, intelligent, and gifted man, who had felt that she lacked the humor necessary to cope with life.

In reply to Esmé's question the soldier said he had not been employed before the war, but thought of himself as a short-story writer. She observed that her father had written beautifully and she was saving his letters for posterity. She told him that the huge watch she wore was a gift from her father just before she and Charles were evacuated. She asked the soldier to write a story for her about squalor, a subject in which she was extremely interested. The soldier delightedly gave her his A. P. O. address when she offered to write him. In parting she wished him a return from the war with "faculties intact."

The squalid part of the story began in Bavaria about a month after V-E day. Staff Sergeant X, one of ten American soldiers in a home in Gaufurt, apparently had not come through the war with his faculties intact. Even after his two weeks' stay at the hospital, he was filthy, trembled, smoked incessantly, and had let a pile of unopened letters and packages accumulate on a table in his room. One day on his return from the hospital he opened a book by Goebbels, *Die Zeit ohne Beispiel* (Time Without Parallel) into which the owner, a minor official in the Nazi Party, had written in German, "Dear God, life is hell." Sergeant X zealously inscribed underneath it Dostoevski's phrase, "Fathers and teachers, I ponder 'What is hell?' I maintain that it is the suffering of being unable to love." He was terrified when he saw that what he had written was illegible.

Sergeant X's fears of his complete collapse were interrupted by the entrance of Corporal Z, with whom he had gone through five campaigns since D-Day. Z's observations and comments on X's nervous breakdown only made X more nervous and unhappy. When Corporal Z finally left the room, Sergeant X, in an effort at therapy, tried to type a letter to a friend in New York, but found his hands were shaking too violently. He put his head down on the typewriter to rest, and when he opened his eyes found a small package. He opened it by burning the string off. Inside was the watch Esmé's father had given her, but with the crystal now broken, and a note from Esmé and Charles dated June 7, 1944. Esmé wished Sergeant X luck, and offered him the watch as a talisman. After looking at the watch for a long time, the sergeant felt happily sleeply. His f-a-c-u-l-t-i-e-s were mending.

Commentary

Of all of Salinger's stories, "For Esmé – with Love and Squalor" is perhaps the most famous and among the most hotly debated. Leslie Fiedler had the courage to call it "a tear-jerker," whereas George Steiner, who is not one of the most voluble of Salinger's enthusiasts, considers it "a wonderfully moving story, perhaps the best study to come out of the war of the way in which the greater facts of hatred play havoc in the private soul."

The truth probably lies somewhere between the two extremes, as it usually does. One may account for the story's popularity in several ways. It is one of Salinger's few attempts, and possibly the only successful one, to come to grips with an obviously significant chapter in contemporary history. If one compares it with the dilettantish religious dabbling in "Down at the Dinghy," Salinger's success here is even more evident. Whereas he escapes resolving anything in "Down at the Dinghy," in "Esmé" one is left with a complete experience, a new perception of historic antagonisms and how they are resolved by a sensitive individual.

The close parallels between Salinger's own experience in the war and those of Sergeant X may account in part for the story's powerful sense of authenticity. The sergeant is presented in four distinct episodes, which together provide sufficient detail for the reader to know him and to empathize with him. In the opening passage Sergeant X is presented as a man who would follow his heart and attend Esmé's wedding, but who is dissuaded from doing so by his "breathtakingly levelheaded" wife. The second episode shows him as he was in 1944, isolated even though in the army, his contacts with the outside world limited to selfish letters from his wife and from his mother-in-law. In the third episode the bright and charming Esmé and the sergeant – two lonely war-haunted figures – reach out toward each other. In the fourth section the sergeant is brought to recovery from battle fatigue in a strangely linked chain of events that included the book by Goebbels into which the Nazi woman had inscribed the bitter condemnation of her life and her world. The sergeant's counter-inscription is an assertion of eternal love, but it is illegible. It is only with the opening of Esmé's package – the tangible gift of love – that his mental wounds begin to heal, and the squalor begins to be eradicated. In a sense, his counter-inscription becomes legible through Esmé.

"For Esmé – with Love and Squalor" is Salinger's most provocative, lucid, and self-contained effort at a universalized statement about life. If it fails to achieve complete universality, the cause may lie in part in the recurrence of certain stylistic tricks of which Salinger is fond. There is a certain cheapening because of the use of specific but not particularly important references to people and places in New York City. And Esmé and Charles, although we may at first accept the narrator's estimate of them, are perhaps a shade too cute, too precocious, too word-loving. If Salinger makes the children in his later stories unbearably articulate and more than just a shade pretentious, Esmé remains credible despite her rather pompous speech patterns. Her sweet voice, her chewed fingernails, her wet hair, and her recalling to the narrator the exact date of their meeting (lest he had forgotten) remind the reader that Esmé is still very much a thirteen-year-old girl. As the narrator points out, Esmé's observations and comments are not those of a smart aleck. Having lost both parents, she thinks of herself as her younger brother's protector. Her conscious mimicking of adult language in phrases such as "I look a fright" is poignant rather than annoying.

Although one can justify Esmé's traits, Corporal Z is a little too loutish to be believed. He wears five bronze stars when he could have worn one silver star. It is hard to believe that Sergeant X could have tolerated him even in his sanest and most benign moments. Corporal Z is certainly present in the story to provide a contrast to Sergeant X, but the farcical elements seem to have triumphed, and the critical reader may find the result damaging to the story as a whole.

In spite of these criticisms "Esmé" is a story that is not easily forgotten. It is a triumph because of what it says rather than of how it is said. Style is subordinated to content – a reversal of the usual formula in Salinger's stories.

"PRETTY MOUTH AND GREEN MY EYES"

Summary

The triangle composed of Arthur, his wife Joanie, and Lee (Joanie's lover and Arthur's law partner) is portrayed nearly entirely through two telephone conversations. These conversations take place in the early hours of the morning after they have all attended a party together. When Arthur first calls Lee, it is obvious that he is quite drunk. His pretext for calling is to find out whether Lee had noticed if Joanie left the party with the Ellenbogens. Joanie lies quietly at Lee's side as he tells her husband that he did not notice her departure. Lee tries to calm Arthur down, but Arthur drunkenly persists in relating his personal troubles – his failure in court that day on an important case, and the failure of his five years of married life, which he portrays alternately as five years with an alley cat and five years with a tender and devoted wife. Arthur attacks himself for being weak, and calls his wife "Madame Bovary at Columbia Extension School." Lee valiantly asserts that he thinks Joanie is a mature woman, but her husband describes her as a "grown *child*." In desperation Arthur asks if he may come over to sit at Lee's place, but Lee firmly advises him to stay at home and call him later if he feels like it.

Joanie praises Lee's handling of the situation, but before their conversation develops, the telephone rings again. It is Arthur reporting that Joanie has just come home. She had been delayed helping Bob Ellenbogen's wife, Leona, get over an embarrassing crying jag. Arthur adds that he has decided that if everything goes along well, Joanie and he will move out to Connecticut, where they can live "a normal goddam life." Arthur tries to return to the topic of the law case he lost that day, but Lee cuts him off, saying he has a headache and will talk to him in the morning. When he hangs up, he does not want to talk to Joanie or to touch her.

Commentary

Salinger succeeds in this story at the tour de force of relating a series of events through two telephone calls. The central subject of the calls, Arthur's wife and Lee's mistress, is scarcely heard from. All that is known of her is learned from her husband's ambivalent remarks and from the fact of her presence at Lee's side. Lee is revealed through a brief description of his appearance and through the words of advice he gives his mistress's husband. Arthur, whose conversations suggest that he is drunken, weak, self-pitying, and isolated, is never overtly described. His valiant lie in the second telephone call helps him to maintain his image of himself. At the same time, it curiously intensifies Lee's sense of guilt, which he had revealed only slightly between the two conversations. As is so often the case with Salinger's stories, the reader is left to guess what will happen the next day. It is as if one had been presented with a very clear action photograph of one instant in the characters' lives, and then been asked to supply all the necessary supplementary information. In other words, what one derives from a sketch of this sort depends largely on what one brings to it. If, for example, one feels that urban society breeds loneliness, alienation, and a fragmenting of human ties, then one will find confirmation of these views in "Pretty Mouth and Green My Eyes." If, on the other hand, one perceives romantic triangles as part of the human condition, one's conclusions might be quite different. Since environment can no longer be blamed for what happens, the individual characters must be held directly responsible for their actions. In interpreting the story from this viewpoint, the reader might keep in mind other literary triangles such as those centering around Francesca da Rimini and Anna Karenina. Since Salinger functions primarily as an observer and reporter in "Pretty Mouth and Green My Eyes," the commentary and conclusions must be filled in by the reader according to his perception of life.

"DE DAUMIER-SMITH'S BLUE PERIOD"

Summary

The narrator, as the young artist, briefly brushes in the background of his story, beginning by explaining that if it made sense he would dedicate the story to his mother's second husband, Robert Agadganian, Jr. His "late, ribald stepfather" was a stockbroker who became an agent-appraiser for galleries and museums in the United States after the stock-market crash. In 1930 the family moved to Paris, where the young artist learned to paint. It was his return to New York in 1939, following his mother's death, that made him miserable. The discovery that he and his stepfather were "both in love with the same deceased woman" prompted him to answer an advertisement of openings for qualified, bilingual art instructors at Les Amis Des Vieux Maîtres in Montreal. Monsieur Yoshoto, supposedly the former director of Tokyo's Imperial Academy of Fine Arts, was head of the school. In applying for the job, the nineteen-year-old narrator used the pseudonym of De Daumier-Smith and stated that he was a widower. His art training in Paris and New York provided him with sufficient skills to devise examples of commercial and fine art.

De Daumier-Smith's sojourn in Montreal was marked by deflation followed by enlightenment. He discovered to his distress that the Yoshotos' art school was in an unattractive part of town. Even though he occupied their absent son's chairless room, he was not welcomed into the family with any warmth. Mme. Yoshoto may have been somewhat more cordial than her husband, but basically the directors were aloof and taciturn. De Daumier-Smith's chores as art instructor included translating M. Yoshoto's critiques of the mail-order students' work into English and criticizing the work of several students of his own. He was not at all impressed by the samples of work submitted by a housewife named Bambi Kramer, or by the efforts of a "society photographer" named R. Howard Ridgefield. The work of a nun named Sister Irma, who taught cooking and drawing at the convent school of the order of Sisters of St. Joseph, appealed to him so much, however, that he wrote her a very long, emotional, and enthusiastic letter. As the days went by, he was oppressed by the necessity of waiting to hear from Sister Irma. Upon looking into the window of the orthopedic appliance shop over which the school was located, macabre notions went through his head:

> The thought was forced upon me that no matter how coolly or sensibly or gracefully I might one day learn to live my life, I would always at best be a visitor in a garden of enamel urinals and bedpans, with a sightless, wooden dummy-deity standing by in a marked-down rupture truss.

The next morning the school received a letter from the Mother Superior of Sister Irma's convent withdrawing her from the course. De Daumier-Smith quickly wrote to Sister Irma urging her not to give up painting; the worst it could do would be to make her a little unhappy. For her benefit, he recalled what had started out to be his happiest day, "many years ago" when he was seventeen (in fact, only two years earlier). On the way to meet his mother for lunch, his great happiness was suddenly dispelled when he was entering the Avenue Victor Hugo and bumped into a man who had no nose. He begs Sister Irma to "consider that factor. . . . It is quite pregnant with meaning." The letter was never mailed.

That evening De Daumier-Smith dressed in his dinner suit and went out planning to celebrate "the tragic occasion" of Sister Irma's withdrawal from the course. He ended up eating in a lunch bar. Walking back to the school, he noticed that a light was on in the orthopedic appliance shop and that a girl was in the window, dressing a dummy. As he paused in front of the shop, De Daumier-Smith had a kind of mystical experience in which he suddenly perceived the window as being full of "exquisite, twice-blessed, enamel flowers." On his return to his room, he wrote in his diary that he was giving Sister Irma her freedom: "Everybody is a nun."

Several days later the school was closed for operating without a licence, and De Daumier-Smith went to spend the rest of the summer with his stepfather in Rhode Island, "investigating that most interesting of all summer-active animals, the American Girl in Shorts." He never resumed his correspondence with Sister Irma, although he still heard occasionally from Bambi Kramer, who had branched out into designing Christmas cards.

Commentary

Before one turns to the critics' rather abundant commentary on "De Daumier-Smith's Blue Period," one should reread this story for the simple, uncomplicated pleasure of watching Salinger the humorist at work. It is possible to read the story as a completely successful and delightfully amusing account of a nineteen-year-old American on the road to self-discovery. Some critics, however, have felt that to read the story on this level is to overlook the symbolism that surrounds De Daumier-Smith's mystical experience. It may be helpful, therefore, to leave the vision of De Daumier-Smith trying to fall asleep with Mme. Yoshoto's dinner riding his "sternum like an elevator" and join the psychocritics and the religious experts to see what they can contribute to our understanding.

The outstanding example of psychocriticism applied to "De Daumier-Smith's Blue Period" is contained in "One Hand Clapping" by Frederick L. Gwynn and Joseph L. Blotner. This essay is included in Henry Grunwald's *Salinger: A Critical and Personal Portrait*. The authors contend that the story is "a humourous treatment of the classic Oedipal situation, wherein redirection of love to a conventional object is surprisingly achieved by means of religious impulse." They have found three "father-figures" in the story: the stepfather, Yoshoto, and Father Zimmerman, a priest attached to Sister Irma's school. They have found love of mother "with its repressed sexual component," and a transferral of love to a nearly adult level of heterosexuality in De Daumier-Smith's affection for Sister Irma. But one should not overlook the castration imagery in the reference to Peter Abelard and in De Daumier-Smith's encounter with the noseless man. Psychocriticism, however, does little for the student that Salinger has not done better or more subtly in the story itself. Salinger, speaking through Buddy Glass, has said elsewhere, "I do cavil . . . with . . . the current ruling intellectual aristocracy educated in one or another of the big psychoanalytic schools. . . . They're a peerage of tin ears."

Other critics regard this story as the first of Salinger's "religious stories," or at least as the portent of a main stream of thought in the best of his later work. Josephine Jacobsen, in an essay included in Grunwald's anthology, classifies De Daumier-Smith's first vision of the orthopedic appliance shop with "the literature of despair." She sees his second view of the shop as the destruction of "the sordid, soulless, hopeless, pointless . . . by the force of the delicate, irresistible infusion: the human exchange of the beatific signals." De Daumier-Smith, with mild irony, refers to this second view as his "Experience."

It is with considerable relief that one returns to the story and notes that although there are indeed psychological and religious undercurrents, they are a natural part of the complicated process of De Daumier-Smith's growing up, which Salinger so skillfully portrays. These undercurrents need not be given symbolic overtones. The hero of this tale is an artistic liar who adopts a series of inspired disguises and deceptions to escape from the grief he feels at his mother's death, at being uprooted and transplanted in New York City, and at being more or less permanently outclassed by his debonair stepfather. As an artist – by definition a hypersensitive person – it is not surprising, nor necessarily part of a serious psychological syndrome, that De Daumier-Smith should be repelled by dentists, crowded buses, noseless men, or orthopedic appliance stores. Each is in its own way a thoroughly disheartening reminder of the human condition and of human frailty. Only when he has come to accept the sordid as a part of life is he able to dispense with his disguises and deceptions and resume the more normal pursuits of a nineteen-year-old boy. By the end of the story the narrator has turned to studying American girls in shorts. The wit and imagination that make this story as good as it is need not be submerged in an ocean of psychoanalytical or religious interpretation to make its author's meaning clear.

"TEDDY"

Summary

The thoughts and actions of Teddy McArdle, a ten-year-old mystic, are not always understood by those around him. His father, a radio actor, becomes enraged when he wakes up to discover Teddy standing on a suitcase, looking out of the porthole at the sea. Ignoring his father's commands to dismount, Teddy calmly philosophizes about some orange peels floating on the water. Another row ensues when Teddy casually informs his parents that he has given his father's Leica camera to Booper, his six-year-old sister. The boy is ordered to retrieve the camera at once.

Teddy finds Booper, a fiendish little creature, making stacks of shuffleboard discs on deck and terrorizing a young companion named Myron. Teddy succeeds in getting Booper to take the camera down to the cabin so that he can be left in peace to write in his diary. As Booper leaves she tells him that she hates him and everybody in the ocean.

Teddy then goes to work on his diary, first rereading a recent entry in which he had encouraged himself to find his father's dog tags to wear them because it would make his father happy. Teddy had also promised himself to write certain letters, to meditate without losing consciousness, and to look up certain words in the dictionary. After reviewing this entry, he makes additional notes. His final statement has ominous overtones: "It will either happen today or February 14, 1958 when I am sixteen. It is ridiculous to mention even."

He is interrupted by a young man he had met in the gym earlier that morning, who had heard one of the tapes Teddy had made for the Leidekker examining group in Boston. After some conversation about the weather, the man introduces himself as Bob Nicholson. In reply to a question about his trip, Teddy explains that he had been interviewed at Oxford and the University of Edinburgh. He also met people from Innsbruck and Stockholm who wanted to see him.

Teddy asks Nicholson if he is a poet (which he is not) and then recites two Japanese poems. Nicholson pursues his own interest in the boy, stating that Teddy had left a lot of disturbed pedants behind him in Boston, including Nicholson's friend, Al Babcock. Teddy explains that he cannot see why others feel the need to get so emotional about things, pointing out that even his notion of love involves only a sense of strong affinity. As an example of imperfect love, Teddy describes his view of parental affection: "They love their reasons for loving us almost as much as they love us and most of the time more." Teddy goes on to clarify for Nicholson some of his ideas on other subjects. He makes it clear that he holds to the Vedantic belief in reincarnation and feels that in another life in India he was "a person making very nice spiritual advancement." He fell from grace in the other life because he had met a lady. Although he was not advanced enough to achieve everlasting death, his fall was a definite setback. As a result of it he was born in America where "it's very hard to meditate and live a spiritual life. . . ." His father finds his mystical inclinations odd, and his mother feels they are bad for his health.

In response to another of Nicholson's questions, Teddy replies that when he was six he had seen that everything was God. This vision of unity came when Booper was drinking her milk, and he perceived that she was God and the milk was God. She was, in effect, pouring God into God. Since the age of four, Teddy had been getting out of "the finite dimension." He painstakingly explains that this transcendence involves abandoning logic – which was in the apple that Adam ate – so that one might perceive the infinite. He denies vehemently that he had ever told any of the professors in Boston the time and place of their deaths, insisting that he merely told them of various times when they should be careful, and of various things it would be good for them to do. Teddy thinks it is silly of them to be afraid of dying – something they had done before, even if they do not recall it. He says that if his sister pushed him into an empty pool and he fractured his skull and died at once, it would be nothing to fear or weep over because it would be what was supposed to happen.

Nicholson reasonably inquires how his parents would feel if he died. Teddy answers that they would be sad, but only because they had certain set responses to all events. In reply to another of Nicholson's questions, he says that children should be educated by having everything their parents taught them emptied out of their heads. In his ideal educational system children would be shown things instead of being given the names for them. They would then begin with things as they are, and not with other people's perceptions or names for them.

Nicholson tries to detain Teddy by asking him more questions, but the young mystic insists on going to his swimming lesson. Shortly afterward, Nicholson hurries down several decks toward the pool. Just as he is descending the final staircase he hears the echoing scream of a small girl.

Commentary

"Teddy" is a transitional story between the well-made tales of *Nine Stories* and the later, more loosely constructed sagas about the Glass family. It may be thought of as an introduction to what Donald Barr has called Salinger's "latest phase." As Barr has pointed out in an essay included in H. A. Grunwald's anthology:

> ["Teddy"] reads *methodically,* as if the impulse had first been to write something that was not a story. It has dialogue of a kind then new to his work but now his standard: no longer seducing our belief and lighting up characters with things we had heard but not listened to, but expounding an ordered set of ideas as plainly as can be done without actually destroying the characters into whose mouths they

are put. The ideas are mostly Zen. The direct, mystical glimpsing of God behind the identities of this world is the way. An unsentimental and unpossessive love is the practical result.

Barr's statement is a helpful summation of Salinger's techniques in this, the last of the *Nine Stories*. Teddy's parents, his sister, and to a more limited degree, Nicholson, are revealed to us through speech mannerisms. As a result, the characters begin to turn into caricatures. Teddy is at once another of Salinger's prodigies and his first genuine seer. De Daumier-Smith's mysticism was, one gathers, only part of a passing phase, whereas Teddy's mysticism directs his past, present, and future.

"Teddy" is perhaps most interesting as a bridge between the inconclusiveness of "A Perfect Day for Bananafish" and the lengthy examination of the events leading up to Seymour's suicide in what we have of the later stories about the Glass family. There are, in fact, some extremely interesting parallels between Seymour and Teddy. Both characters came to a violent end. Both foresaw that their days were numbered and proclaimed the fact. Both accepted the foreknowledge of their death with apparent composure because of their philosophies. Both felt that their beliefs and habits set them apart as seers.

In "Seymour: An Introduction," Buddy Glass explains that the eyes are the most abused part of the true artist-seer's anatomy. The artist-seer "is mainly dazzled to death by his own scruples, the blinding shapes and colours of his own scared human conscience." The reader, then, should not be perplexed to find the author making so much of the fact that Teddy was cross-eyed. It would seem that Salinger is not so much cherishing the peculiarities of his characters, as he is often accused of doing, but using these deviations from the norm as a symbolic device. In any event, Seymour and Teddy are intended as representatives of the small class of true artist-seers, from whom we are apparently intended to learn. If there is an academic intention here, it fails, partly because we have been conditioned to think of suicide as the weakling's way out, rather than the strong man's eagerness to reach Brahma and eternal peace. The intention fails because one is puzzled by Seymour's and Teddy's real motivations. In both cases we know enough about their immediate families to suspect that they might find death preferable to living in such a setting. This is especially true of Teddy who may reasonably be described as schizophrenic on the basis of the evidence contained in the story. In short, the reader's credibility may be overly strained by Salinger's efforts at putting the words of Zen scholars into the mouths of babes.

One's acceptance or rejection of Teddy may also hinge on one's age. The younger one is, the more likely one is to applaud his theory that parents love their reason for loving their children more than they love the children themselves. Parents – even the most detached and rational ones – are not likely to swallow that pat observation easily. Even though Teddy's contemporaries might find it amusing to experiment with his learning-by-seeing method, they are not likely to regard him as anything but a poor freak once he has launched into his theory of intellectualism and logic as the source of original sin. Right or wrong, however, Teddy's views are so strongly at variance with the fabric of Western thought that any effort to portray them may be doomed from the start. The reader wants to cry out, "We are only ordinary mortals! Don't go so fast." There may be an important message for us in "Teddy," but it is imperfectly delivered.

The ending of the story, for example, is just vague enough to have caused almost as much public concern as "Franny" did when it was first published in *The New Yorker,* and half of the magazine's readers went around asking the other half whether or not Franny was pregnant. "Teddy" ends in such a way that one is left asking, "Did he fall or was he pushed?" The consensus is that he was pushed. Nicholson hears a shrill female scream, and Booper has been set up as a virulent, jealous creature with innumerable motives for destroying her strange sibling, just as Teddy predicted she might. Given the vagueness of the ending, however, the reader may wonder whether Teddy was mentally unbalanced enough to set Booper up as his potential destroyer in Nicholson's mind, and then kill himself by jumping into the empty pool when he knew Booper would be there to take the blame. Given this latter possibility, Teddy would become one of the most repulsive animals in recent fiction, a candidate for a long voyage with the nasty twins of Katherine Anne Porter's *Ship of Fools.* The evidence is strongly against this vicious alternative, however, simply because Salinger seems to like Teddy so much.

The reader, limp from not being sure just what has happened in "Teddy," will at least find relief and support for one conclusion in H. A. Grunwald's fine parody of Hilaire Belloc's *Cautionary Tales.* Grunwald entitles his parody "Teddy McArdle, Who had Strange Powers and was cut down to Size by his Sister."

> . . . And then (oh jealous Little Fool!)
> His Sister pushed him in the Pool,
> Suceeeding with the first Attempt. He
> Was not surprised to find it Empty.

> MORAL

> Bright Little Boys who play with Zen
> May not grow up to be Big Men.

Critical Appraisal

The well-intentioned critic must approach Salinger's work with considerable concern. The most obvious reason is that any judgments one makes about a living author must be modified as more of his work appears. This is especially true about Salinger, whose audience, it has been said, awaits new additions to the history of the Glass family with the same eagerness and intensity that made Dickens' enthusiasts go down to New York harbor to meet the boat carrying the last instalments of the *Old Curiosity Shop.*

Dickens' readers were eager to learn the fate of Little Nell. The publication of new additions to the Glass-family saga can perhaps be compared even more aptly to the publication of Lawrence Durrell's *Alexandria Quartet*. As each new novel in the *Alexandria Quartet* was published, it completely overturned the tidy conclusions drawn at the end of the preceding novel. Similarly, we cannot be too certain about where Salinger is leading us in the story of the Glass family, let alone how long their narrative will continue to preoccupy him.

The enormous volume of criticism that has already appeared is another reason for caution. Virtually every major American critic as well as an impressive collection of educators, psychologists, and sociologists have had their say. There has been so much critical interest in Salinger partly because his creations have won a loyal following, particularly among high school and college students, who seem to establish some kinship with Salinger's portraits of young people. The stories themselves reflect some aspects of contemporary life so faithfully that their inclusion on required reading lists in various courses seems quite natural.

Salinger also has had his say about Salinger. His tone is sometimes plaintive, sometimes ironic. The dedication of *Raise High the Roof Beam, Carpenters and Seymour: An Introduction* reads as follows:

> If there is an amateur reader left in the world – or anybody who just reads and runs – I ask him or her, with untellable affection and gratitude, to split the dedication of this book four ways with my wife and children.

In "Seymour: An Introduction" the conversation between the author and his "fairweather friend, the general reader" is continued at some length. Salinger includes the whimsical offering of an "unpretentious bouquet of very early-blooming parentheses" to his readers for not being, among other things,

> . . . unskilled guitarists and Zen-killers and incorporated aesthetic Teddy boys who look down their thoroughly unenlightened noses at this splendid planet where (please don't shut me up) Kilroy, Christ, and Shakespeare all stopped. . .

Then follow some extremely well-made and sharp comments aimed at students of "aesthetic pathology," inhabitants of the "busy neo-Freudian Arts and Letters clinics," and other "prosperous camp followers of the arts."

"The amateur reader" does exist, but Salinger seems to overlook the fact that his stories are so constructed that the amateur reader will probably read and run, and then run back to reread his stories. In the *Nine Stories* Salinger has so much to say that seems relevant, and that is, in general, so brilliantly well-expressed. It is not surprising, or for that matter alarming, that the reader ultimately loses his amateur standing. He may not be able to play in Salinger's Olympic Games, but there is reason to suspect that the manager would not be too distressed after all.

One Hand Clapping

The epigraph for *Nine Stories* is a Zen koan:

We know the sound of two hands clapping.
But what is the sound of one hand clapping?

Salinger's average reader on the rerun will surely return to these lines and puzzle over their relationship to the stories. The relevance of this koan to *Nine Stories* has been summarized neatly by Gwynn and Blotner in an essay in Grunwald's anthology:

> To the merely literary, this might appear comic, possibly some echo of the Krishna ceremony in Forster's *A Passage to India,* where the Hindu Godbole lays down one cymbal so that he can adjust his pince-nez, while with the other cymbal he clashes the air. To the merely critical, the saying might stimulate symbolic application to the stories, with something made of the isolation, the "one hand clapping," of Seymour, Eloise and so many others. But students of comparative religion would recognize this as the most famous of the seventeen-hundred-odd koans of Zen Buddhism, those surrealistic unanswerable conundrums designed to stir up and readjust one's view of things. "Zen has always specialized in nonsense," Aldous Huxley puts it, "as a means of stimulating the mind to go forward to that which is beyond sense . . ." A koan thus makes a perfect epigraph for a writer who wishes to entitle his book of nine stories *Nine Stories:* the reader has not to apply the quotation *to* the tales but simply to be thereby aware that the tales present problems which he may or may not solve for himself by supersensory perception.

William Wiegland, in an essay included in Grunwald's anthology, has observed wryly that "Salinger's Zen is to the faithful like Shelley's Platonism – vague and a little dry." The applicability of this statement to *Nine Stories* is not difficult to understand. The only spokesman for what might be called the Zen outlook is Teddy McArdle in the last story. Teddy is such an uncomfortable personality that one is tempted to discard Zen along with him into the empty swimming pool, where one is supposed to believe that he found fulfillment – the true spiritual life that is divorced from material concerns – in death. According to this view, death is not an end but a desirable entrance to a freer and better state. At least as far as *Nine Stories* is concerned, the ideas of Zen should probably not be overstressed. An expression such as epiphany, which James Joyce used to describe the sudden insight and the sudden revelation of relationships and meanings, will do as well to emphasize what Salinger is trying to do in these stories. As the reader considers the significance of Salinger's stories, he begins to perceive characters and events in a fresh way. The koan is a way of directing the reader's attention, and not necessarily an encouragement to join the ranks of the mystics. In an essay that appears in Grunwald's anthology, Dan Wakefield has summarized the role of mysticism in the *Nine Stories:*

> Though many of Salinger's characters are concerned with mysticism, Teddy is the only real mystic, and his particular answer is not the answer for any other characters and does not provide an answer to Salinger's search . . . The search of his fiction moves from Teddy's mystical withdrawal from the world to three long stories that chronicle a pilgrim's progress into that world.

It would not be too far-fetched, however, to point out that the pilgrim's progress may have been portrayed as early as Eloise's exit from Ramona's bedroom in "Uncle Wiggily in Connecticut," and that it is certainly the theme of "For Esmé – with Love and Squalor" and "De Daumier-Smith's Blue Period." It should also be noted that in each of these stories the inaudible "one hand clapping" gives promise of becoming an audible "two hands clapping." It is in "Esmé" that this affirmation of life receives its clearest and most effective expression. Sergeant X travels the spiritual distance from the Nazi woman's desperate outcry of "Dear God, life is hell," to the Dostoevski-inspired perception that hell "is the suffering of being unable to love."

Each of the *Nine Stories* can be analyzed in terms of the characters' search for love. Even the less important stories such as "Just Before the War with the Eskimos" and "Down at the Dinghy" portray the struggle of people who are trying to build a bridge to another human being for whom, to use Teddy's words, they "have a very strong affinity." It is these strong affinities in their various states of growth and repair that link the nine stories in the collection, and are perhaps responsible for the stories' continuing importance to readers. Since we are all pilgrims in pursuit of wisdom, the reader may find reflections of himself in Salinger's prose.

A Flawless Eye

Seymour Krim has called Salinger "a romantic with a flawless eye." Salinger's feeling for the nuances of language and gesture is remarkable. In each of the *Nine Stories* the description of some seemingly trivial gesture is magnified to reveal the character's true state of mind. An obvious example is the description of Jean De Daumier-Smith's first encounter with M. Yoshoto:

> It was a bus ride of several miles from Windsor Station to the school. I doubt if M. Yoshoto said five words the whole way. Either in spite, or because, of his silence, I talked incessantly, with my legs crossed, ankle on knee, and constantly using my sock as an absorber for the perspiration on my palm.

Salinger never seems to waste any words in pinning down a character. Corporal Z's odiousness in "For Esmé – with Love and Squalor" is underscored when Salinger tells the reader that "His brick-red hair, just combed, was dripping with the amount of water he required for satisfactory grooming." Salinger is just as proficient at portraying the awkwardness of adolescence. His description of Ginnie in "Just Before the War with the Eskimos" perfectly captures her lack of grace.

> At fifteen, Ginnie was about five feet nine in her 9-B tennis shoes, and as she entered the lobby, her self-conscious rubber-soled awkwardness lent her a dangerous amateur quality. It made Selena prefer to watch the indicator dial over the elevator.

One has only to glance at Charles's antics in "For Esmé – with Love and Squalor," or at Ramona's noisy galoshes in "Uncle Wiggily in Connecticut," to recognize that Salinger has an eye for the very young as well.

It is a commonplace to praise Salinger's dialogue for its flawless reproduction of contemporary sounds. He has preserved all the awkward little notes with which adolescents punctuate their speech and the patent phoniness that peppers their parents' conversations. We know just how interested Mary Jane is in meeting Ramona when she says "Oh, I'm dying to see her," or how many different things are going on simultaneously in Joanie's head when she tells her lover in "Pretty Mouth and Green My Eyes" that he was "Absolutely marvellous" on the phone. A study of Salinger's dialogue reveals how frequently hyperbole ("breathtakingly levelheaded," "immoderately perceptive") and italicized words appear in the daily speech of our time. In the short story a remarkable amount of background description can be omitted if the characters sound believable when they are talking – and Salinger's do.

In *Nine Stories* there is very little purely descriptive writing. A location, a detail of decoration or clothing, and an occasional word about the season or the weather are all the description that is generally given. The word "sketch" as applied to these stories is more understandable when one realizes just how deftly the few lines of background are drawn. David L. Stevenson, in an essay in Grunwald's anthology, has described the Salinger short story as "a kind of closet scene between Hamlet and his mother with the rest of the play left out." Since the story generally focuses on two or three important characters at a critical point in their lives, its impact upon the reader depends on a "frugal underplaying of plot" and a "minimizing of narrative."

Peter Pan on Park Avenue?

Salinger said in his biographical note in *Harper's* in 1949, "I almost always write about very young people." Sybil in "A Perfect Day for Bananafish," Ramona in "Uncle Wiggily in Connecticut," the narrator in "The Laughing Man," Lionel in "Down at the Dinghy," Esmé and Charles in "For Esmé – with Love and Squalor," and Teddy in the story "Teddy", are all part of Salinger's well-known collection of precocious young people, of whom the most famous member is Holden Caulfield.

Salinger's preoccupation with the young has led critics to accuse him of fleeing from reality, of creating child saviors and monsters of precocity. Critics also see this preoccupation with youth as symptomatic of a cultural revolution in which the loudest voice in our land is that of the adolescent. Salinger's young people have been compared to virtually every other child in literature, from the biblical Jesus to William Golding's and Richard Hughes' isolated murderers. When all the possible stimulating comparisons have been made, the question must be answered as to whether Salinger's preoccupation with children is similar to Sir James Barrie's treatment of children in his sentimental *Peter Pan*. In *Peter Pan* the good children line up with the fairies to get away from adult domination. Or is Salinger's interest in young people intended as something of more depth and consequence?

It has been pointed out that Salinger's children are looking for some object worthy of their love. In seeking to form strong affinities, they encounter every variety of adult indifference and phoniness. The search of these children may strike an adult, who has abandoned or buried the need for that search, by its innocence and directness. It is obvious that the adults who survive in Salinger's stories are the ones who have responded to the proffered gift of love that seemingly springs from the child's intuitive, uncluttered vision. As H. A. Grunwald has said:

> It is surely no accident that in so many civilizations, the child, like the fool, is assigned a special oracular authority. Nor can this be dismissed simply as superstition. It is part of mankind's collective experience that out of the mouths of the young can come truth and that in the eyes of the young, the world is new . . . All of Salinger's work is imbued with this belief . . .

Not all readers are moved by the role assigned to children in Salinger's work. Some protest that he carried the idea of the "child savior" too far for comfort, and that such characters as Esmé, Teddy, and Sibyl are a little too cute, too splendidly verbal, and altogether too special to be borne, or believed. Others have complained that the range of his characters is limited. Most of his characters are Easterners – Manhattanites by birth – and all seem to belong to the upper middle-class that attends private schools, Ivy League colleges, and travels to Europe. They are what is loosely described as privileged. As a result, Salinger has been accused of performing like a hypnotist, wing-walker, or ventriloquist.

There is really no answer to these protests because one either goes along with an author's creations, or one does not. It does seem, however, that Salinger often bends over backwards to make his young people seem real and ends up making them appear more than a little uncouth, bad-mannered, or overwhelming. One thinks of Ramona's nose-picking, Esmé's flinging herself at the soldier, and Teddy's philosophizing. The reader senses Salinger pushing a good thing too far – a failing that has become noticeably pronounced in the more recent stories about the Glass family, which John Updike has accused Salinger of loving more than God himself loves them. It may be simply that most readers respond negatively when the virtues of a person are enumerated endlessly without any substantial evidence of those virtues.

Sibyl, in a "Perfect Day for Bananafish," may have been Seymour's last experience of happiness, but it should be noted that she is not a terribly fetching child. She is just a shade selfish and pushy. Similarly, Esmé may save Sergeant X, but is (with abundant reason) quite impressed with herself. None of this would warrant any comment at all were it not that Salinger's work is full of children whom he seems to want us to love as he does, perhaps simply because they are children. This does not seem reason enough. An occasional protest by an adult who cherishes whatever hard-won maturity he has gained, even in exchange for innocence, may be permitted as yet another acned adolescent or runny-nosed child emerges as a near saint.

Perhaps the most sensible statement that has yet appeared on the subject of Salinger's preoccupation with the young is Warren French's. In the concluding portion of his study, *J. D. Salinger,* French suggests that the

> . . . school of thought to which Salinger (and many other writers for *The New Yorker*) appears to belong stems not from the wise and witty Sir James Barrie, but from a fictional character whom William Wiegland identifies with Salinger and Salinger himself mentions in "A Girl I Knew" – Goethe's young Werther. Like Salinger's Seymour, Werther shoots himself. Before his demise, however, he says, "Children are nearer to my heart than anything else on earth," and argues that we should treat them, "as God treats us – He makes us happiest when he lets us wander under the intoxication of agreeable illusions . . . ." Such intoxication, is, however, incompatible with mature achievement, and as long as Salinger remains under its influence – as he is when he writes about Seymour Glass – his art is likely to deteriorate. There is more than mere "envy" in Norman Mailer's observation that Salinger is "the greatest mind ever to stay in prep school."

*J. D. Salinger: The Mirror of Crisis

Salinger is surely one of the most skillful practitioners of the *New Yorker* short story or sketch. And, invidious critics aside, his sketches show it to be, at its best, one of the truly distinctive and definable fictional types of mid-century American letters. This kind of story contains no more than two or three characters, seen always at a moment of crisis in one of their lives. The concentration is on the crisis: the relationships which have led to it are indistinct, only suggested by the tone of the dialogue, by characters' momentary actions and gestures. The Salinger-*New Yorker* story is always a kind of closet scene between Hamlet and his mother with the rest of the play left out. It accomplishes its shock of surprise, and it evokes our emotions, by a frugal underplaying of plot and event, by its very minimizing of narrative. The reader is usually not projected into the problems of its characters because he is not given enough of the fabric of their lives to make such projection possible.

*By David L. Stevenson. From *The Nation*, CLXXXIV (March, 1957).

What a Salinger story *does* involve the reader in is something quite different. It is his awareness that the crisis of the sketch is a generic one of our time and place. The crisis of the usual *New Yorker* story may be fairly casual, and we have come to expect a Salinger story to be more stern in its implications because its roots are stronger and probe more deeply. But its crisis runs true to form. Salinger does not take you out of yourself into a living, substantial world of fiction. He throws you back into your own problems, or into an awareness of them in your contemporaries. His characters do not exist in a rich narrative, in a detailed setting, so that they become wholly separable, fictional beings. Rather they give us a feeling of our own sensitivity to compensate for their lack of created density.

One can best illustrate this quality of a Salinger story by comparing his *New Yorker* sketch "Pretty Mouth and Green My Eyes" with Hemingway's "The Short Happy Life of Francis Macomber." The two stories offer the same basic character relationships: passively suffering husband, aggressively lustful wife, and casual, opportunistic lover. In Hemingway's version, however, the characters are embedded in a full, complex plot in which motive and event are made inexorably overt. The tensions of the characters are in open balance for the reader, and the husband's declared failure of nerve is what provokes his wife's ruthless retaliation in taking a lover. The Macombers exist in the round as "created" individuals in a self-contained narrative which could be translated into mandarin and remain comprehensible.

Part of the virtue of "Pretty Mouth and Green My Eyes," on the other hand, is that it is not a self-contained narrative. We know of the characters only that they are apartment dwellers in New York. They exist as voices on a telephone to illustrate the desperate irony of a husband calling his wife's latest lover, after a party the three of them have attended, at the moment when the lover is in bed with the wife. The tearing crisis of the story is the husband's slow realization, as he complains in hideously maudlin, drunken terms of his wife's infidelities, that he has put his own self-respect beyond the point of salvage. Salinger's characters, here, come alive *New Yorker* fashion through the skillful verisimilitude of their conversation. But, like E. B. White's famous figure in "The Door" (also untranslatable into mandarin), they have social rather than narrative roots. They are important to us in direct proportion to our recognition of them as generic sketches of our urban, childless, apartmented men and women, alienated by the hectic nature of their lives from all quiet interflow of love and affection.

One significant element in the structure of a Salinger story, then, and a source of his power over us, is that his characters come alive in our recognition of them. In complementary fashion, an equally significant element is the effect on us of the special kind of crisis he asks us to identify. As in "Pretty Mouth and Green My Eyes," it is a crisis in a character's life that results from an erosion of personality peculiar to upper middle-class, mid-century America. It is related to our sense of the heightened vulnerability of men and women to emotional disaster.

I am not prepared to argue that the Salinger species of crisis is unique, and that other ages did not feel themselves alienated from inner security and outward affection. *Hamlet* alone would suffice. I should only assert that in our time and place the individual estranged from his fellows seems peculiarly understandable and therefore touching to us. If one needs outside documentation, I cite the fact that no age but our own has found a partial picture of itself in such a sociological study of estrangement as David Riesman's *The Lonely Crowd*. It is not that we, as a generation, are defeated, or without will. Perhaps it is merely that our religion, our family ties, our cultural traditions now give us a lighter armor than our predecessors wore.

At any rate, Salinger's fiction convicts us, as readers, of being deeply aware of a haunting inconclusiveness in our own, and in contemporary, emotional relationships – members all of the lonely crowd. His characters exist outside the charmed circle of the well-adjusted, and their thin cries for love and understanding go unheard. They are men, women and adolescents, not trapped by outside fate, but by their own frightened, and sometimes tragi-comic, awareness of the uncrossable gulf between their need for love and the futility of trying to achieve it on any foreseeable terms.

Salinger's short stories are all variations on the theme of emotional estrangement. In "Down at the Dinghy," a small boy runs away when he overhears his father referred to as a "kike." In "Uncle Wiggily in Connecticut," two women, unsuccessful adventurers in love, let a Connecticut afternoon drift away on highballs and reminiscences, while the timid child of one of them retreats farther and farther into compensatory fantasy as the two women get progressively more sodden. In "A Perfect Day for Banana Fish," a young soldier released from an army hospital confronts his wife's complicated indifference during their first reunion. When he is forced to weigh a small child's warm, intuitive sympathy against his wife's society prettiness, he shoots himself. The actions of the characters in all these stories could seem arbitrary, judged by the sketchiness of Salinger's narrative. In fact, however, the actions seem real and shocking because they are the kind of thing we can anticipate from the needs and stresses we share at least in part with the characters.

Salinger's most ambitious presentation of aspects of contemporary alienation, and his most successful capture of an American audience, is in his novel *The Catcher in the Rye*. It is the brief chronicle of Holden Caulfield, a sixteen-year-old boy who escapes to New York after flunking out of his third prep school. The novel is written as the boy's comment, half-humorous, half-agonizing, concerning his attempt to recapture his identity and his hopes for belonging by playing a man-about-town for a lost, partially tragic, certainly frenetic weekend. *The Catcher in the Rye* is a full-length novel, and yet gives much the effect of his shorter pieces. Its dimensional depth is extrinsic to the narrative, and is measured by the reader's response to the dialogue, and the background of city America. It is supplied by one's recognition that Holden Caulfield, sensitive, perceptive, is too aware of the discrepancies between the surface intentions and the submerged motives of himself and of his acquaintances to feel at ease in any world. Through him, Salinger has evoked the reader's consciousness of indefinable rejections and rebellions that are part of the malaise of our times.

As we have come to expect from Salinger's other work, the main devices of character in *The Catcher in the Rye* are an apparently effortless verisimilitude of dialogue and an unerring sense of the appropriate in details of gesture, of bodily movement. There is a further fictional device, used elsewhere in his short stories, but of paramount importance in his novel in creating a hold on the reader. It is his use of almost Chaplin-like incidents and dialogue, half-amusing, half-desperate, to keep his story always hovering in ambivalence between comedy and tragedy. Whenever a character approaches hopelessness in a Salinger sketch, he is getting there by the route of the comic. It is usually both the character's way of holding on for a moment longer (as when the husband in "A Perfect Day for Banana Fish" goes out of his way to insult a proper dowager just before he kills himself) and, at its sharpest, a way of dramatic irony, a way of heightening the intensity of a character's predicament (as when Holden attempts to be bored with sex to get rid of a prostitute). But no single scene from his novel completely demonstrates this peculiar strain of comedy in Salinger: it pervades, seeps into, almost every incident.

When one is reading Salinger, one accepts his carefully placed "New Yorkerish" style and tone, and surrenders one's mind almost completely. It is only when you put the story aside and turn to other contemporary writers and to other fictional methods and techniques that you begin to wonder whether the immediacy and vividness of Salinger might be limited in power. Nowhere in Salinger do we find ourselves plunged into the emotional coiling and recoiling provoked by passages from Styron's novel, *Lie Down in Darkness*. Nowhere in Salinger is a character moved against the murky intensity-in-depth of a Nelson Algren Chicago scene, in *The Man with the Golden Arm*. Nowhere is a character revealed by the great clots of heterogeneous detail yoked together in single, crowded sentences, as by Saul Bellow in *The Adventures of Augie March*.

But despite the temptations of comparison there remains one's conviction that Salinger is deeply and seriously committed in his fiction. Further, a little research into the Salinger canon reveals that two of his major creations, Holden Caulfield and Seymour Glass, the young husband of "A Perfect Day for Banana Fish," have deep roots in Salinger's own imagination. His novel, in its way, is as much a final version of "work in progress" as are the novels of his more literary contemporaries, pulled together from fragmentary excursions as short stories in *Partisan Review*, in *Hudson Review*, in *New World Writing*. Only with Salinger, the professional, early sketches of Holden Caulfield occur in a series of stories published in *The Saturday Evening Post*, *Collier's*, and in *The New Yorker*, in the years 1944-1946. And Seymour Glass turns out to have rich inter-connections in Salinger's mind with the uncle of the runaway boy of "Down at the Dinghy," with the older brother of the heroine in a sketch "Franny" (*New Yorker*, January 29, 1955), and with the bridegroom in a novelette *Raise High the Roofbeam, Carpenters* (*New Yorker*, November 19, 1955).

This extrinsic information helps verify one's feeling that there is actually more weight to his explorations of human alienation than his bright dialogue and his frugal use of background and event might suggest. Moreover, Salinger's non-literary status leaves him, as a serious writer, almost unique as a wholly free agent, unhampered by the commitments of his more dedicated contemporaries to one or another school of critics. One might guess that this is Salinger's most precious asset. Rather than wishing quarterly significance or "greatness" on him, we can be content to take him for what he is: a beautifully deft, professional performer who gives us a chance to catch quick, half-amused, half-frightened glimpses of ourselves and our contemporaries, as he confronts us with his brilliant mirror images.

Suggested Study Topics

The Catcher in the Rye

In order to achieve a more enlightened and comprehensive view and evaluation of *The Catcher in the Rye* the following study topics and/or assignments are suggested for the reader's use.

1. The vernacular speech of Holden Caulfield has been described as producing an effect that is "half humorous and half agonizing." To what extent does the author use hilarious situations with serious undertones to develop his novel?

2. List five instances in the novel that illustrate Caulfield's compassion for some of his colleagues.

3. Would you consider Holden Caulfield's criticism towards the "phonies" as mature or does his point of view suffer from a failure to compromise with the way things are? Why is it important for Caulfield not to compromise in order to preserve his own standards and integrity?

4. What are the qualities that Holden sees in the nuns that make their charity work different from that of his mother's friends?

5. What makes Holden's language unique and how does it contribute to the characterization and pace of the novel?

6. Do you consider Caulfield a misfit or would it be more accurate to say that it is his society that is left of center? Which view do you share and why?

7. Compare Salinger's approach to the adolescent world with that of any of the following writers: F. Scott Fitzgerald, Booth Tarkington, Mark Twain, Saul Bellow.

8. To what degree do you consider *The Catcher In the Rye* as serious literature?

9. What is the significance of Caulfield's concern for the ducks in the lagoon in Central Park?

10. J. D. Salinger has been called the most representative voice of the present student generation. What is it that has earned him this title in terms of view and presentation?

Nine Stories

1. Arthur Mizener has suggested that "Salinger's short stories are all variations on the theme of moral estrangement." Do you agree? Support your point of view in an essay.

2. The idea of the child as savior seems to recur in several of Salinger's short stories. Discuss this theme in terms of any three of the *Nine Stories*.

3. Some of Salinger's stories seem to be constructed along theatrical lines. Using "A Perfect Day for Bananafish," "Uncle Wiggily in Connecticut," and "To Esmé – with Love and Squalor" discuss the stories in terms of acts – natural, suspenseful breaks in the narrative – where the curtain might be lowered. Do you think the stories gain or lose in tension because of this construction?

4. Salinger's use of dialogue is often praised for its authenticity and credibility. Do you agree or disagree with this praise? Support your viewpoint by using examples from the *Nine Stories*.

5. The quotation from Dostoevski in "To Esmé – with Love and Squalor" is sometimes offered as a key to all of Salinger's stories. Why? Do you think it is the best key? Are there others, and if so, what are they?

6. Salinger's *Nine Stories* seem to focus on a rather limited segment of society in the northeastern United States, but his popularity is worldwide. What accounts for whatever universality he possesses as an author, in spite of his limited focus?

7. Leslie Fiedler has suggested that Salinger presents madness "as the chief temptation of modern life, especially for the intelligent young. . . ." Do you feel that Salinger follows this course, and, if so, which of the *Nine Stories* support this contention?

8. Compare and contrast Salinger's portrayal of Lionel Tannenbaum, Sybil Carpenter, Charles, and Ramona Wengler. What do they have in common? How are they different? Do they support the view that Salinger is at his best writing about these young people?

9. The epigraph of *Nine Stories* is a Zen koan (or riddle): "We know the sound of two hands clapping. But what is the sound of one hand clapping?" What does this mean, and how is it appropriate to the collection?

10. Which of the *Nine Stories* do you consider the best and why? Discuss in

detail the reasons for your choice, comparing the story with others in the collection.

Bibliography

Barr, Donald. "Saints, Pilgrims and Artists", *Commonweal,* LXVII (October, 1957).

Branch, Edgar. "Mark Twain and J. D. Salinger: A Study in Literary Continuity", *American Quarterly,* IX, No. 2, Part I (Summer, 1957).

Browne, Robert M. "In Defence of Esmé", *College English,* XXII, No. 8 (May, 1961).

Corbett, Edward P. J. "Raise High the Barriers, Censors", *America,* (November 19, 1960).

French, Warren. *J. D. Salinger.* New York: Twayne, 1963.

Galloway, David D. *Absurd Heroes in American Fiction: Updike, Styron, Bellow, Salinger.* Austin: University of Texas Press, 1970.

Grunwald, Henry Anatole, ed. *Salinger: A Critical and Personal Portrait.* New York: Harper and Brothers, 1962.

Gwynn, Frederick L., and Blotner, Joseph L. *The Fiction of J. D. Salinger.* Pittsburgh: University of Pittsburgh Press, 1958.

Hassan, Ihab H. "Rare Quixotic Gesture: The Fiction of J. D. Salinger", *Western Review,* XXI (Summer, 1957).

Jacobs, Robert G. "J. D. Salinger's *The Catcher in the Rye:* Holden Caulfield's 'Goddam Autobiography' ", *Iowa English Yearbook.* (Fall, 1959).

Leitch, David. "The Salinger Myth", *Twentieth Century,* CLXVIII, 1005 (November, 1960).

Lundquist, James. *J. D. Salinger.* (Modern Literature Monographs) New York: Ungar, 1978.

McCarthy, Mary. "J. D. Salinger's Closed Circuit", *Harpers,* CCXXV (October, 1962).

Reiman, Donald H. "Holden in the Rye", *College English,* XXIII, 6 (March, 1962).

Seng, Peter J. "The Fallen Idol: The Immature World of Holden Caulfield", *College English,* XXIII, 3 (December, 1961).

Simonson, Harold P. and Hager, Philip E. *Salinger's "Catcher in the Rye" Clamor vs. Criticism.* Boston: D. C. Heath and Co., 1963.

Wisconsin Studies in Contemporary Literature, IV, No. 1, (Winter, 1963).

NOTES